I0620488

MENTAL MOGUL MINDSET

*Key Strategies for Achieving Mental
Clarity and Leadership Success*

DR. LORETTA CULBREATH COLEY

Cocoon to Wings
PUBLISHING

MENTAL MOGUL MINDSET
Copyright © 2024 Loretta Culbreath Coley

Printed in the United States of America
ISBN: 978-1-963964-05-9 (Paperback)
ISBN: 978-1-963964-06-6 (Digital)

Library of Congress Control Number: 2024908291

Published by Cocoon to Wings Publishing
7810 Gall Blvd., #311
Zephyrhills, FL 33541
www.CocoontoWingsBooks.com
(813) 906-WING (9464)

Scriptures marked with the designation "GW" are taken from GOD'S WORD®. © 1995, 2003, 2013, 2014, 2019, 2020 by God's Word to the Nations Mission Society. Used by permission.

Scriptures marked NIV are taken from the HOLY BIBLE, NEW INTERNATIONAL VERSION® (NIV®): Copyright ©1973, 1978, 1984, 2011 by Biblica, Inc.® Used by permission. All rights reserved worldwide.

Scriptures marked NKJV are taken from the HOLY BIBLE, NEW KING JAMES VERSION®. Copyright © 1982 by Thomas Nelson. Used by permission. All rights reserved.

Scriptures marked NLT are taken from the *HOLY BIBLE*, NEW LIVING TRANSLATION, Copyright © 1996, 2004, 2015 by Tyndale House Foundation. Used by permission of Tyndale House Publishers, Inc., Carol Stream, Illinois 60188. All rights reserved.

Book cover design by ETP Creative

MENTAL MOGUL MINDSET

*Key Strategies for Achieving Mental
Clarity and Leadership Success*

PREFACE

This book addresses the behaviors associated with success using critical parameters related to mental stamina and supportive actions. The book introduces the concepts of mind mapping, the bragging factor, and the Master Key theory. The processes demonstrate how individuals think about achievement, perceptions, and the behaviors needed for a healthy focus. The book also attempts to address the *LeaderMind* theory and key behavioral components that directly affect achievement. The Mental Mogul Mindset practically identifies constructs that individuals and organizations can use to create structured leadership development plans through literary analysis and human-based social research. The results of the study further clarify the concepts of the *LeaderMind* theory and its application. The book reflects behaviors and actions that individuals can use to begin constructive development, leading toward success.

ACKNOWLEDGEMENTS

I am thankful to God for sustaining me during my academic studies and affording me the opportunity to utilize my divine gifts to write this book.

This book is dedicated to my husband (Kevin) and daughter (Harmony) for their unfailing love and support.

I am grateful to my late parents and know that they would both be proud of this work, as it was their goal for me to receive the best education possible.

I am also thankful to my late grandparents and all those who have tirelessly poured into my potential and existence, as I express those investments through a life lived out loud.

To my siblings, in-laws, and extended family, I am thankful for your prayers and support and hope to always represent you well.

I offer many thanks to the Regent University faculty, students, and friends who have supported me on this journey.

I would also like to extend a special thanks to those who participated in this book's research and completion.

Without **all** of you, none of this would be possible.

FOREWORD

Mental Mogul Mindset offers strategies that can be applied to one's personal or professional life, especially if you want to find a balance between the two. Leaders are tasked with providing the vision and implementing action steps to ensure success for all. Whether it's mental discovery, Master Key thinking theory, *LeaderMind* theory, or any of the other theories, concepts, or strategies discussed in depth in Mental Mogul Mindset, Dr. Coley provides practical and applicable explanations of each.

In addition to Dr. Coley's sharing of personal experiences throughout the book to allow you to resonate with what you are reading, it is befitting that her book includes mental moments for you to immediately partake in immersing yourself in the strategies. Whether you view your personal or professional life as reaching a destination or enjoying a journey, Mental Mogul Mindset can equip you to achieve what you desire.

Dr. Rhonda D. Ray, EdD
Federal Programs Director
Owner-Success Unlimited Solutions, LLC
Aiken, South Carolina

In Dr. Coley's words, "This book demonstrates a suitable course of action to build personal beliefs and create disciplined behaviors that drive individuals toward their God-given desires and achievable results." She builds a practical component on existing research as she invites the reader to join her on this journey towards achieving your own personal best in mental focus and clarity.

Dr. Coley took a tried model of organizational change and applied it to the individual. This is a huge development on this model and her work in doing so is sound and contributory. This book takes a deep dive into the thinking, thoughts, and thought patterns of the individual and how they must change if change is to take place. She covers mental fortitude, purposes and patterns, training, supportive networks, and perseverance. Dr. Coley notes, "Self-control translates progress into success." She closes each chapter with thought-provoking questions that will help individuals develop their strategies for change and determine where to go from here.

Throughout the book, Dr. Coley uses biblical integration in forming and expressing her thoughts. She weaves in family values and the legacy of her grandparents throughout. She is transparent as she uses her own story to further develop the practicality of the model she is presenting.

Dr. Diane M. Wiater, PhD
Adjunct Professor
Regent University-School of Business and Leadership
Owner-Wiater Consulting Group, LLC
Cincinnati, Ohio

Dr. Coley's book is filled with assessments, tools, and techniques designed to achieve the level of mental acuity necessary to attain personal and professional success. Drawing from extensive research, she builds greater awareness of the critical role our thinking processes play in building barriers to success or in serving as bridges to overcome the obstacles holding us back. As she repeatedly affirms, the difference between success or failure is typically a matter of how we view and think about our circumstances and our drive to take deliberate "right action." These lessons are echoed in a framework of scripture woven throughout the book with a synchronization of the psychological and scriptural compliments required to adopt the *Mental Mogul Mindset*.

Once we learn how to get out of our own way, we can then begin the process of picking up our Master Key to unlock opportunities previously locked away from us. A bedrock of the book draws from the *LeaderMind* theory coupled with tools such as positive habits, skill-building, focus, self-care, guidance, and correction. Dr. Coley's book has wide application for all types of leaders in many business sectors and especially for those determined to move on from the ordinary to extraordinary business and life success!

Dr. Virginia Richardson, BCC
Adjunct Professor of Strategic Foresight, Leadership and Healthcare
Regent University-School of Business and Leadership
Champaign, Illinois

CONTENTS

CHAPTER 8 SUCCESS AND INTENTIONS — 125

TABLES

FIGURES

BOOK INTRODUCTION

S tamina is a critical element when it comes to the balance of business concepts. The innovative techniques of engineers can often go against maintaining a strategic posture in the complex field of global marketeering. A slight twist of the wrist and a whole business system's tumbling blocks can falter causing massive repercussions not quickly congealed in the rebuilding process. However, on the verge of a maniac obtrusion lies the creative precipice that can foster something new, engaging, and so fanatically different that it calls attention to itself without even trying. The opposite is also true. The abridging forces delve into the unknown with a vengeance for balance that brings the ordinary and comfortable into the light of visionaries' past. This emotionally charged action leaves the seemingly unchallenged foe of innovation in the exposed morning of equilibrium, quenching it of any drive towards unleveled success. The result is a life of lackluster quality filled with no determination and an unsuccessful mindset. The mind is mysterious, and its actions and behaviors avow for the success of what seems right at the time, even if what seems right is wrong for the individual. However, as creative forces in God's image, we have an essential role to play, both as innovators of our future and reconcilers of our past. The only bridge between the two is discovered in the mind, and the goal of our futures takes place on the sequestered platform of an unbroken bridge of networks that constitutes our ability to drive success and achieve the desires of our hearts.

Mental Mogul Mindset

Unfocused individuals try to calm their internal motivation in the middle of an unabridged highway stacked with foes that challenge the concept of right and wrong. This thinking process is much like the overstimulated parent seeking refuge from the constant bombardment of parental responsibilities and personal desires. The only escape for both may be to retreat to a bubble bath of bliss or an uninterrupted nap in the middle of the day. The idea behind the Mental Mogul Mindset is to understand the balance between aspirations, identifying the tools needed to accomplish success, and finding the courage and stamina to implement strategies and adjustments in reaching the desired goals required to achieve success. There is no result without the ability to go into one's treasure chest of desires and fears and plunge headfirst into the reckoning of achievement. That reckoning begins with the passion for a headstrong knight challenged by the opposing force of the heavily armored dragon. The successful mogul dominates the forces that are needed to accomplish change. They rise to the challenge and bring defeat to the imagined, or sometimes real foe, by achieving what many only ever dream of - personal success that outweighs obstacles while dreaming and focusing on the only reality it understands. This reality begins in the mind and plays out in the tangible. The aim of the Mental Mogul Mindset is to change this reality and is the reason to start this quest.

Where do I begin? This is the question that plagues many who desire more remarkable results in life. Business success starts with the individual. What do you hope to achieve, and how will you get there? The process of reaching objectives begins with how people think. How people feel about constructs originates with internal messaging. But what determines self-esteem or stamina or the ability to achieve the goals patterned before us? How does a young girl from Mississippi living below the poverty line become an Oprah, or a business owner starting a small-town garage become a Jeff Bezos? What sets these individuals apart from others? Alexander Lyod discusses mental capacity as an attitude of positive affirmations and willpower in his book, *The Love Code*.[1] However, what determines the steps that precede the affirmations or the first steps toward success? How does an individual transition from the couch to the corporate executive seat? These questions stem from the idea that there is something that precedes goal-setting and the actions needed to initiate success. As a business professional, I have made many attempts to successfully strategize new businesses and exceed previous quests. I am learning from those around me that business success and success in life (in general) start

---

[1]   Alexander Lyod. *The Love Code: The Secret Principle to Achieving Success in Life, Love, and Happiness.* (New York: Harmony Books, 2015), 3, 75.

from a specific place located inside the mind. Perhaps you selected this book because the title intrigues you. If that is the case, I could assume that you would like to know more about achieving success based on mental focus. I wrote this book with you, the leader, in mind. I hope that it allows you to think more clearly about how mental focus affects the choices that lead to success in life. I also hope that you find practical uses to achieve your next goal with greater ease. Ultimately, this book demonstrates a suitable course of action to build personal beliefs and create disciplined behaviors that drive individuals toward their God-given desires and achievable results.

I Dream; therefore, I Achieve

The dreamer awakens to become the improviser and connoisseur of all things and all knowledge when they realize who they are. Many successful questers begin their lives on the open tyranny of the playground. The ability to achieve the unimagined lies deep within the forces of thought coupled with passion. A young girl imagines herself as a princess, and voila'; the outcome of concepts, mostly founded in imagination, leads to the desired practice of royalty only limited by the child's ability to conform to their imposed surroundings of time and parental guidance. Left unchallenged, this princess goes on to become the queen of her kingdom and those in her vicinity. As a quick heads up, I will be referencing several biblical passages

> **THE DREAMER AWAKENS TO BECOME THE IMPROVISER AND CONNOISSEUR OF ALL THINGS AND ALL KNOWLEDGE WHEN THEY REALIZE WHO THEY ARE.**

- from my position as a person of strong faith – to clarify understandings. Ephesians 5:14 reminds us to awaken and become all that we are meant to be in life.[2] The same awakening is true for those who genuinely seek to find personal success. Looking deeply within unveils the small pieces that can drive success forward. However, looking at oneself with such candor can also release suppressed emotions, especially triggering for those who wish to avoid certain realities. Embracing all parts of the process can additionally lead to the acceptance of self and others who have helped shape and mold the core of our existence. The possibilities are endless. Because the world is so diverse and everyone that makes up our global patchwork so unique, understanding your individualized core foundation can take much more time than this book can offer. Looking beyond the text will offer the needed time to strategize the type of commitment to achieve long-term, desired results. With this aim in mind, I challenge you to read this book at least twice. Once to get acquainted with the theories or concepts it proposes, and then as necessary to implement strategies. If the concept of reading a book twice seems abstract or weird to you, think about it in terms of watching your favorite movie repeatedly to get to the best scene in the film; except approaching this book more than once may lead you to experiencing breakthroughs and accomplishing the desires that lead to your success.

The mental machine is complicated. It can drive some insane while leading others to brilliance. Capturing the

---

2   Eph. 5:14 (New International Version).

essence of that mechanically organic wonder is the aim of this book. Capitalizing efforts to achieve personal success can create myriads of opportunities in private success ventures and provide a roadmap for successful leaders to follow. From the onset, mapping this concept has been a discovery of pathways that lead down varying roads. However, the paths always lead back to the same origin: where does it all begin, and how can it be modified if it does not suit the needs of the individual attempting to change? The questions 'where' and 'how' may make a person behave in abstract manners. How can personal achievement drivers operate to overcome challenges of self-image, belief, and environmental factors? Where is the path to discovery that will lead an individual down the path to success ownership? These additional questions are a part of a patchwork, much like quilting. The story of success constructs one piece, block, or concept together at a time. Understanding this process is even more critical as it will determine the strategies and the timeline for making short-term commitments that can lead to lifelong success. I invite you to join me and many others on this journey towards achieving your own personal best in mental focus and clarity. Welcome to the winner's circle, the Mental Mogul Mindset.

Book Outline

This book is segmented into 10 chapters, introducing leadership theories that induce record-time achievements. Each chapter concludes with thought-provoking questions that help develop strategies for change and determine where to go from here. These inquiring sections are small mental breaks designed to challenge your thoughts. I have never been one who has particularly enjoyed journaling. However, I encourage you to use a journal to document individual answers to the summary questions, allowing you to get the most out of this book as a useful resource. Otherwise, enjoy the journey of reading, and when you are ready to apply the details, come back to the most relevant sections.

Chapter One begins with the introduction of mental discovery and what makes individuals think the way they do. It further details the process of cognitive development for adolescents into the behaviors expressed as an adult. This chapter also addresses self-image for leaders and the concept of purpose as a derivative foundation for mental growth and achievement. The chapter questions thought processes, comfort levels, and internal drivers toward success.

Chapter Two discusses the importance of understanding your foundation. It reaches into the depths of personal behaviors that lead to success. It also answers the question of how we define success and how we should relate to obstacles in life. This chapter further discusses the key to unlocking everything you desire to achieve in life by examining the Master Key Thinking theory. Unleashing your potential begins with the ability to relinquish control and abate feelings of doubt and fear. The reading challenges individuals to act to see the results that they desire. The question of personal drivers leads to the discussion of self-belief in Chapter Three.

Chapter Three discusses how personal belief systems are formulated, how they affect individuals, and what it means concerning mental focus and achievement. Words are discussed as primary indicators of steering actions and beliefs when creating value and nurturing relationships. Finally, mental stamina and success link to the discussion of perseverance.

Chapter Four lays the groundwork for achieving success based on the *LeaderMind* theory.[3] The concepts related to establishing a framework of behaviors that support mental focus are discussed, including five pillars that leaders can use to build others in their organizations.

Chapter Five leads the discussion on the use of tool kits and how valuable they are to an individual's focus. The first toolkit approaches the use of habits, skills, and focus as postulates in achieving success.

Chapter Six translates the second wave of tools focusing more on self-care ideals, external guidance, and self-correction. Individuals learn the importance of steering their path and using the tools that create balance on their journey to success.

Chapter Seven demonstrates the vital pillars of the *LeaderMind* theory in practice.[4] Testing the *LeaderMind* hypothesis provides valuable insight when using a framework that acts as a guide for individuals to achieve success

---

3   Loretta Coley, "Developing the Global Leader Mindset". LDSL 733. *Regent University*, Unpublished Essay, 2020.

4   Coley, 2.

with minimum obstacles.[5] The *LeaderMind* theory is tested within the constructs of a specific timeframe, allowing better focus and analysis of the ideas related to achieving success while delivering unexpected thoughts and outlays related to achieving goals[6]. Results-driven research describes and discusses the behaviors that individuals and organizations should use related to the use of the *LeaderMind* theory.[7]

Chapter Eight discusses intentions versus actions and how the two concepts can collaborate to help individuals achieve goals. Developing the mindset to achieve based on decisions is discussed as the first action step to achieving success and shifting the mind from stasis to movement. It also addresses the ability to connect with your internal passions and transition those ideas to reality.

Chapter Nine discusses the use of mentorship and coaching. It addresses the key aspects of a successful mentor or coach and provides key paradigms that individuals can use to determine whether they need a mentor or a coach to help them achieve their goals.

Chapter Ten breaks actions into process steps and allows an individual to transcribe vision into strategic reality. The chapter discusses the mold that surrounds achieving success and how mental focus breaks the barriers that can hold an individual captive by unleashing potential.

----

5   Ibid.
6   Ibid.
7   Ibid.

CHAPTER 1

DETERMINING YOUR INTERNAL STATE, YOUR STARTING POINT

> "Human nature is to need a map. If you are brave enough to draw one, people will follow." ~Robert Louis Stevenson.[8]

I have always been fascinated with maps. Before the concept of digital maps arose, I owned several Rand McNally maps, an uncommon feat for a nineteen-year-old on the quest to drive as many places as my new economy Ford Escort would take me, of course, without getting lost. However, there was one thing that the maps could never deliver: the next unexpected adventure or the discovery of a new area. Living near the Chesapeake Bay coast most of my life, I could never have imagined that my young adult years would form in a location that I mistakenly stumbled upon on a trip home one 4th of July. As a sailor in the Navy, I cherished my downtime. Every opportunity I could get, I would hit the road to see people, places, and things. I followed my map closely as I left my military duty station in Norfolk, Virginia, and set out on a quest to reach home in cozy South Carolina for the long holiday weekend. However, I quickly realized that maps could

---

8   Robert Louis Stevenson. AZ Quotes. (n.d.) Accessed February 17, 2020. https://www.azquotes.com/quotes/topics/maps.html.

not do what navigation now can, which is to redirect you quickly. Missing my first significant exit thrust me into what I assumed was a wilderness adventure through a massive underwater tunnel to nowhere. I later realized it was the Monitor Merrimac Memorial Bridge-Tunnel, that allowed me to encounter a future destination of my foundational path. It was among this massive outlay of undeveloped forestry and farmland that I would later settle and begin my family. Many years later, when my husband and I purchased our first home as a young couple near the Chesapeake Bay, I remembered my misadventure with a brief chuckle of how unintentionally veering off the map could lead to beautiful discoveries.

Simply put, maps are essential. Plans put things into perspective and help us understand where things are and, in some cases, what they mean. However, understanding how to use them in the discovery process is more important than the map itself. A map legend could explain a thing or two. Also, understanding the scale of the drawings places items into context. If I know my favorite gas station is five miles away and my car is running low on fuel, map icons can help me decide my next move. However, some of the best discoveries are made when we create our path or discover a new way to drive to the neighboring town. After all, if the Wright Brothers had never left the boundaries of what was tangible, they would never have reached the impossible realization of human-crewed flights. Just imagine travel today without the use of airplanes; that's a lot of holiday time spent trying to get to a destination.

Mind Mapping

The concept of ***mind mapping*** begins with understanding how a person thinks and grasps personal goals. The thinking grid uncovers layers of thoughts influenced by culture. Environmental factors are just one part of the thinking process. Just as chemicals react with their environments, thoughts mix with our environments to formulate unabridged areas that can affect our lives' trajectory. This theory relates to how people think and why.

Figure 1-1 Mind Mapping Model

As a theory, the process of thought begins with how we enter the world. We start as malleable plush, absorbing the things around us and interacting through processes. A great example is the process babies experience. A baby feels discomfort from a wet diaper and begins to cry. A parent attends to the crying baby, and the child learns to think in terms of cause and effect. The baby understands that crying equals attention and, eventually, comfort. Although this is a basic level of thinking, the concept is the same throughout life. In business, external factors and strategy are primary indicators of resulting success, as noted by Den Born and Van

Witteloostujin in the 2013 *Journal of Organizational Behavior.*[9] We could impose the same logic regarding personal success, where the external factors relate to culture, and the strategy refers to how we translate or react to the cultural influencers. In the book *Developing Thinking and Understanding in Young Children: An Introduction for Students,* Sue Robson refers to the cultural interactions children perceive as differences in social contexts based on geographical locations during adolescence.[10] Robson further suggests that social contexts determine individual success factors concerning the dynamics of a child's cultural environment.[11] She also brings light to the subconscious awareness of self-observance in relation to the integration with others as a necessary means to future development.[12] These perceptions add to the theory of consciously deciding how to think and the process of environmental mixing with social expenditures, resulting in forming an individual's thoughts.

A foundation of understanding supports the historical thinking value, giving credence to how we think, feel, and act when we are in specific environments or around certain people. One of the most popular used proverbs, 'When in Rome, do as the Romans,' as referenced by Hanzén in the

9   Arjan Van Den Born and Arjen Van Witteloostuijn. "Drivers of Freelance Career Success." *Journal of Organizational Behavior* 34, no. 1 (2013): 42.

10   Sue Robson. *Developing Thinking and Understanding in Young Children: An Introduction for Students.* (London: Taylor & Francis, 2006).

11   Ibid, 41.

12   Robson, 42.

article coining the phrase in its title, "When in Rome, Do as the Romans Do: Proverbs as part of EFL Teaching," comes to life where tapping triggering factors may cause individuals to act in a resulting way.[13] The question regarding the behavioral choices that people make creates a whole list of exploratory areas. Some people can enter a horrible environment and persevere. At the same time, others may find themselves at the mercy of their surroundings and falter in a way that causes them to achieve less as time goes on. Yuill and Little suggest a strong connection between the language children uncover during their formative years and resulting behaviors later expressed in life depicted in the 2018 *British Journal of Educational Psychology*.[14] The relationship between human development and social behaviors further suggests the value placed on cultural norms and environmental influences. Language and its effects on adult behavior can provide a path forward for those striving to make effective changes that drive success.

Intrinsic Motivational Factors

In his book *The Love Code*, author Alexander Lyod also describes achievement in terms of the intrinsic factors that

---

13　Maria Hanzén. "When in Rome, Do as the Romans Do: Proverbs as a Part of EFL Teaching." PhD. diss., Jönköping University, DiVA (2007): 28, 29.

14　Nicola Yuill and Sarah Little. "Thinking or Feeling? an Exploratory Study of Maternal Scaffolding, Child Mental State Talk, and Emotion Understanding in language-impaired and Typically Developing School–aged Children." *British Journal of Educational Psychology* 88, no. 2 (2018): 264.

drive people toward success.[15] Lyod embraces the idea of finding internal passion when determining the behavioral aspects that govern people.[16] Concepts that make us feel good result from internal factors.[17] However, could the answer to what drives motivation be that simple? Going back to the baby and the wet diaper, could it be that the baby simply wants to feel good? And do we associate wishing to achieve success as an adult with the idea of doing what feels right?

Montag et al. reference Maslow's Hierarchy of Needs while addressing several factors that point to the direction of success drivers.[18] Understanding Maslow's chart concerning motivation leads to the top level of self-actualization.[19] Figure 1-2 depicts a connection between intrinsic factors and the resulting behaviors that create a human propensity to achieve more in life. This awareness level demonstrates the relationship between extreme success expressed in individuals beyond basic personal needs.[20] Charting the path to success may not always be as clear and is contingent upon personal factors that differ among individuals.

---

15   Loyd, 34.
16   Loyd, 34-35.
17   Ibid, 37-38.
18   Christian Montag et al. "Linking Individual Differences in Satisfaction with each of Maslow's Needs to the Big Five Personality Traits and Panksepp's Primary Emotional Systems." *Heliyon* 6, no. 7 (2020): 1.
19   Montag et al., 1.
20   Ibid, 1.

MASLOW'S HIERARCHY OF NEEDS

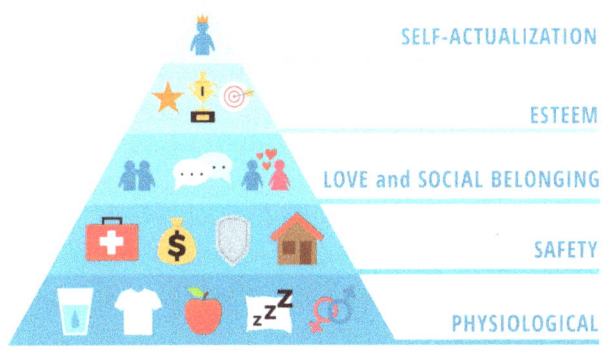

SELF-ACTUALIZATION

ESTEEM

LOVE and SOCIAL BELONGING

SAFETY

PHYSIOLOGICAL

Figure 1-2 Maslow's Hierarchy Of Needs
(iStock Photo: Sabelskaya)[21]

The ability to achieve success is not only based on environment and social needs. The ability to connect ideas in a meaningful way validates the ability to affect change in the lives of those around us. And what about those internal concepts and how they relate to affecting others? According to Amitai Etzioni in the article "The Moral Wrestler: Ignored by Maslow," behavioral research suggests that people are predetermined to make individual choices resulting in specific outcomes.[22] Etzioni also introduces the concept of hedonistic, or self-intrusive factors, that lead people to desire outcomes based on the meaning of what brings them relevance and

---

21   Sabelskaya. 2022. "Maslow's Pyramid, Hierarchy of Human Needs, Vector Flat Illustration on White Background." Accessed on April 15, 2024. https://www.istockphoto.com/vector/maslows-pyramid-hierarchy-of-human-needs-vector-flat-illustration-on-white-gm1396894083-451501313

22   Amitai Etzioni. "The Moral Wrestler: Ignored by Maslow." *Society* 54, no. 6 (2017): 514.

satisfaction.[23] However, this line of thinking, where moral concepts lead to behavior constructed on personal gain, leaves out the idea of selfless acts. Selfless acts, such as those countless good Samaritans helping others following the terrorist attack in New York City on September 11, 2001; Army rangers protecting fellow soldiers during war; or strangers assisting other motorists when danger is present on treacherous highways, each reflects ways that people give of themselves without desiring anything in return. Another way to think about this phenomenon is that **people want to matter, which is the bottom line.**

We are consciously and subconsciously thinking of ways to matter to our bosses, families, environments, and ourselves. Understanding this underlying current is the beginning of creating success that satisfies us and those in our circle of influence. Steven Covey (1989) discusses 'logotherapy,' or the self-discovery of life's meaning, in his book, *The 7 Habits of Highly Effective People:*

> "In the Nazi death camps where Viktor Frankl learned the principle of proactivity, he also learned the importance of purpose, of meaning in life. The essence of 'logotherapy,' the philosophy he later developed and thought, is that many so-called mental and emotional illnesses are really symptoms of an underlying sense of meaninglessness or emptiness. Logotherapy eliminates that emptiness

---

23   Ibid, 512-513.

by helping the individual to detect his unique meaning, his mission in life."[24]

The Purpose of Me

Purpose brings clarity and opens the door to meet greatness with action. An individual's purpose is essential in defining mental clarity because it sets the path to follow. The issue is that many individuals define their meaning based on selfish ambitions and material goals. Proverbial scriptures support this understanding: 'Beauty is fleeting' and the adage, 'this too shall pass' reminds us that nothing lasts forever.[25] So, what matters in the quest for lifelong dreams? Rick Warren has dedicated a whole series of writings to this very topic. In his book *The Purpose Driven Life: What on Earth am I Here For?* he details a person's ability to surrender as a critical factor for identifying and achieving purpose in life from the perspective of God as the processor:

> If God is going to do his deepest work in you, it will begin with this. So give it all to God: your past regrets, your present problems, your future ambitions, your fears, dreams, weaknesses, habits, hurts, and hang ups. Put Jesus Christ in the driver's seat of your life and take your hands off the steering wheel. Don't be afraid; nothing

---

24 Steven R. Covey. The 7 *Habits of Highly Effective People: Restoring the Character Ethic.* (New York: Free Press, 1989), 109.

25 Prov. 31:30 (NIV).

> under his control will ever be out of control. Mastered
> by Christ, you can handle anything.[26]

Our ability to surrender the change process makes us impressionable pieces of artwork that can be molded, shaped, guided, and delivered. We may make our plans, but God provides the course of direction that will lead to real success.[27] Understanding this makes us champions before we begin. To successfully lead and achieve, we must start by following others. The same is valid for achieving mental clarity and focus. Consider the biblical mandate of Mark 12:17: 'Well then,' Jesus said, 'give to Caesar what belongs to Caesar, and give to God what belongs to God.'[28] The scripture suggests that the things reserved for God are for him alone. This thinking is also correct as it relates to the purpose that we follow in life. The ability to surrender also allows room for mentorship, where those with experience can assist you in reaching your full potential.

The Bragging Factor

From childhood, we are taught to act in humility, meekness, and self-gratitude. This way of thinking means that putting ourselves out front is not always seen as necessary as being able to observe from the background. Countless success leaders stand out front. They are humble in nature, and many guide from a posture of extreme gratitude. However, success

---

26   Rick Warren. *The Purpose Driven Life: What on Earth am I Here For?* (Grand Rapids, MI: Zondervan, 2002), 83.

27   Prov. 16:9 (NIV).

28   Mark 12:17 (New Living Translation).

and leadership go hand in hand with platform living. Feeling comfortable in the spotlight is one of the feelings that successful people must embrace. While it is possible to lead from the background, persuasive leaders are known to stand out, even if it is just in their followers' minds. Michel-Kerjan proposes this idea as truth in his article "Effective Risk Response Needs a Prepared Mindset," suggesting the requirement to lead from the front for many in leadership roles, especially those such as politicians who seek to form collaborative relationships among strategic initiatives that affect their constituents' livelihood.[29] The propensity to stand out is complementary to accomplishing tasks that require others to follow.

Standing in the forefront requires an acceptance of who we are so that we can confidently share those details with others. However, when was the last time that you bragged about yourself to yourself? Maybe you were standing in front of a mirror and said some positive things to the individual in the reflection. Try this exercise: **write down 10 things about yourself that make you feel proud. Stand in front of the mirror and read the list aloud with confidence**. Now, call up a friend and share the same list. That was not so hard, was it? Are you comfortable enough to share the same list with your boss? This action may not be so easy for many people. Why isn't it? Some may think of this as selfish behavior rooted in egotism. Why do we think that bragging is selfish? Maybe it's because of cultural upbringings that encouraged us to base ourselves on a false sense of humility. However,

---

29   Erwann Michel-Kerjan. Effective Risk Response Needs a Prepared Mindset. *Nature (London)*, 517, no. 7535 (2015): 413.

humbleness and self-confidence are not mutually exclusive. Mother Theresa was confident that she could help others. She did so out of an abundance of selfless acts. Nevertheless, she challenged others to give as she did. To be successful, we must be comfortable with thinking of ourselves differently, in a successful way.

Marianne Williamson shared her philosophy on confidence based on overcoming the fear of success. 'Our deepest fear is not that we are inadequate. Our deepest fear is that we are powerful beyond measure. It is our light, not our darkness that most frightens us,' [as cited in Elain Partrow's book *The Quotable Woman, Revised Edition: The First 5,000 Years* (p. 702)].[30] And what if we are so successful that we can't help but brag about ourselves? Does that mean that we are less humble? No, it simply suggests that people recognize the qualities they are developing and can be more than they ever thought they could be.

In his book *No Excuses: The Power of Self-discipline*, Brian Tracy encourages readers to move toward fear, not away from it.[31] In these spaces, we can see our self-confidence manifest and balance exhibited in our lives.[32] The conclusion demonstrates a positive effect from self-confidence, the removal of doubts that plague the mind, and the freedom to make necessary changes in life. Multiple encounters of fear may present

---

30   Elaine Partnow. *The Quotable Woman, Revised Edition: The First 5,000 Years*, Facts on File Library of Language and Literature (New York: Facts on File Inc., 2011), 702.

31   Brian Tracy. *No Excuses! The Power of Self-discipline*. (New York: MJF Books, 2010), 112.

32   Tracy, 112.

themselves in life. Having the confidence to face those forces head-on can begin the track to building self-confidence. As we move further, we will explore this topic in detail and illustrate the contingencies to building a life of discipline to help overcome life obstacles.

Belief in the Workplace

For the business professional, the corporate setting can be a daunting challenge with its complexities situated among understanding the key players' mindsets in the work environment. Daily changes in staff, literal and mental, and business practices bring an onslaught of additional issues for those hoping to accomplish big goals. You may formulate the ability to achieve the mindset required by learning to be comfortable with being uncomfortable. However, being uncomfortable comes with rewards. Brian Tracy shared a three-part formula for becoming successful at work that sums up the comfortability discussion: 'Come in a little earlier, work a little harder, and stay a little later. This will move you so far ahead of your competitors that they will never catch up.'[33] The snowball effect that meets the challenge of small ideas can create an overwhelming benefit of returns. Large corporations often develop from these smaller goals or ideas.

Steve Jobs accomplished big goals for humankind, according to research by Walter Isaacson.[34] While embracing technology, such innovators require a brandish personality

---

33   Tracy, 138.
34   Walter Isaacson. "The Real Leadership Lessons of Steve Jobs." Harvard Business Review, 90, no. 4 (2012), 94.

that allows the ability to stand out among others. Jobs' innovative ideas surrounding the communication, electronics, and entertainment industries are cause for applause. However, Jobs' passions were once met with rejection when he was expelled, then brought back into the Apple empire.[35] Over time, Jobs' consistency and focus proved beneficial in his ability to lead others beyond their comfort levels.[36] Dedication to oneself can lead to practical thinking based on understanding one's potential.

To Live or To Die?

How do individual characteristics affect the process of thinking and self-actualization? The moment a person begins their life journey, they are progressing. That progression is either leading them toward their life mission or away from it. To exist in limbo is to neither live nor die. Being in limbo is not a place where people would likely want to find themselves. Making the connection to progress no matter the environment is the mark of a great achiever. The story of Olympic gold medalist Marion Jones brings with it the highs and lows of personal success and seemingly failures. Ron Rapport reflects on the athlete's journey in his book *See How She Runs: The Making of a Champion,* sharing that Jones' childhood was wrought with disappointments from her mother's death, being raised by others who did not necessarily value her worth or talent and having to push herself

---

35   Ibid, 94.
36   Ibid, 98, 100.

during struggles in her adolescence.[37] Her driving force moved her past her disparities and into the arena of multiple Olympic Medals and a career that surprisingly seized her passions and helped her realize her goals.[38] Marion Jones understood how important it is to complement the mindset with big dreams. The visionary mindset can achieve feats that ordinary thinking may find strange or absurd. Leaning on the ability to think creatively offsets the challenges that obstacles present.

Shifting from Reality to Creativity

Living in everyday realities can be viewed as the basic and superficial aspects of life. It refers to common behaviors such as brushing your teeth, lacing your shoes, and folding the laundry. The realities of achieving success can be just as crucial as the mobilization of innovative strategies that initiate positive outcomes. How does that relate to common behaviors? Folding your clothes may seem like a menial task at times. However, feeling good about your wardrobe as a result of successfully completing your laundry can result in increased confidence. Increased confidence radiates during your work presentation, then your stellar work is spotlighted in front of the CEO. That may eventually result in a promotion during the next business cycle. If folding my clothes might lead to a promotion, that puts completing the laundry into a new perspective.

---

37   Ron Rapoport. *See How She Runs: Marion Jones and the Making of a Champion.* (Chapel Hill: North Carolina: Algonquin Books, 2000), 9-16.
38   Ibid, 85, 204.

Combining the realities with results is the same as achieving success. Success achievers put in the work. They understand that the mental focus needed to achieve success depends on their ability to tap into the resources that eliminate obstacles in the thinking process. They also deliver impactful results that incorporate the minimal behaviors that lead to more precise mental focus and clarity for a change. The method of becoming a mogul in any area is to master the effects that challenge the process and deliver results amidst a myriad of environments.

This process of achieving success is built in stages through layers of various accomplishments and growth levels. Tracy further supposes that when it comes to achieving success in the workplace, demonstrating above-average effort yields better results.[39] Specific achievements require a small number of disciplined inputs. However, for extreme success initiatives, such as those brought on by what Jim Collins and Jerry Porras call BHAGS (big, hairy, audacious, goals), the expectancies to include mental fortitude can create a capacious list of requirements and calculated motivators for achievement.[40] Aligning your thoughts to reach huge goals can work in favor of big accomplishments.

Mental Moments: Where do we go from here?

This chapter should help you start to reflect on many areas of mental focus and clarity. Visiting the initiating factors

39   Tracy, 139.
40   Jim Collins, and Jerry I. Porras. *Built to Last: Successful Habits of Visionary Companies.* (New York: Harper Collins: 1997), 93-94.

related to how people think and the individual factors of success development, such as internal drivers and being comfortable with the ability to stand out, are just a few

THE ABILITY TO ACHIEVE SUCCESS STARTS WITH ACHIEVING *WISDOM* AS A PRIMARY FOUNDATION.

of the areas addressed throughout this book. The additional strategic criteria will meet the challenges to the theory surrounding success behaviors and personal achievement. The ability to achieve success starts with gaining wisdom as a primary foundation. Proverbs 4:7 reminds us that in everything, understanding should be the primary focus of what we hope to achieve in life.[41]

Franklin Covey (1989) gives insight on wisdom:

> Wisdom is your perspective on life, your sense of balance, your understanding of how the various parts and principles apply and relate to each other. It embraces judgement, discernment, comprehension. It is the gestalt or oneness, an integrated wholeness.[42]

Meeting the goal of mental focus requires individuals to understand how they currently think and why. This understanding combines cultural inputs and behavior. When we begin to understand the process of change, more remarkable successes will follow. Further insight will allow individuals to determine better how other artifacts, such as self-image, affect achievement. Selecting a focus further expands the concept

---

41   Prov. 4:7 (NIV).
42   Covey, 109.

of deciding what is essential in an individual's life. Relying on God's ability to provide in every area, including the idea of success, is the foundation of how one can begin to develop strategies for achievement.

The onset of the mental champion process starts with vital questions.

Understanding the answers to the following questions develops a starting path to success by breaking apart the initial mental focus areas and allowing changes to those areas that do not serve the ability to achieve goals.

- Do you understand your mind's map?
- Are you ready to become your best self?
- What are your internal drivers?
- Are you comfortable with being uncomfortable?
- Can you define your purpose?

Now that the foundation for mental discovery has started, it is time to address the components of success that affect mental focus and how each supports the other. The foundation of anything is the beginning. The result always points back to how something started. Initiate the process well.

CHAPTER 2

STRENGTHENING THE FOUNDATION

> 'Lock your secret within you in joy, confident and happy that some day you will bear the son of your lover by expressing and possessing the nature of your impression.' ~ Neville Goddard (p. 101).[43]

The Heart of Me

Sometimes, my heart beats erratically. Is that a scary feeling? Well, yes, it is. However, it's one of those challenges in life I must observe and overcome. My faith is so strong that I can often think my heart back into rhythm. On the rare occasion when my heart fails to respond to my thoughts or becomes overwhelmed, I take medication as a last resort. Over several years, I have experienced medically induced or electro-cardio conversions in the emergency room to restore my heart rate to a healthy pace. When I was younger, I found myself in several scenarios where others were suffering medically. At the age of 10, I remember watching my grandfather have a debilitating seizure. Those early experiences drove my desire to become a doctor. Though years later, I realized how much I dislike needles and the sight of blood, and let's say that reality ultimately altered my path. I still took the journey

---

43   Neville Goddard. *The Power of Imagination*. (New York: Tarcher Perigee, 2015), 101.

toward becoming a doctor, just one that did not involve blood or wearing scrubs, though I highly commend those who do.

What I have learned about myself is I have a strong foundation of faith. My culture groomed me to walk on that path. Others around me made sure that I was in Sunday school, Bible study, Saturday worship, Sunday evening worship, vacation Bible school, church pageants and programs, and a part of the youth choir. I remember wanting to sit in the middle row of the church pews to rest on the wall and take a nap when I was sleepy. I also wanted to sit far away from the church mothers. These were the older women who would wake you up and send you to the back of the church to get a drink of water if you were falling asleep during church service. These childhood stories are funny now. However, they constructed a solid foundation that built many skills that I have been able to use in life. Public speaking, initiated as a skill in my adolescence, from formal presentations before the congregation to reciting scriptures or poems, has led to my role as a professional facilitator. Playing football with the older neighborhood kids and attending a high school with students from varying socioeconomic backgrounds allowed me to relate and communicate well with others, no matter their upbringing. Of course, I have built upon these skill sets over the years. However, I know where they began, on that humble country church road back in the 1970s. Of course, you, too, have built your foundational skills. However, have you ever taken the time to identify what your past has taught you and how you can use it to propel you into your future?

Foundational Lessons

We can learn from many different resources. Life teaches us a lot if we are willing to listen. Our paths dictate patterns in our behavior and help formulate how others think about us.[44] The question may remain: why understand our background? And how can understanding our past make a difference if it already occurred? Well, the short answer is our past matters to our future. Through observing our history, we become more astute about who we are as individuals and the criteria that determine our behavior. In the book *The Secret to Success: The Three O's That Will Take You Anywhere in Life*, Samuel Chand refers to understanding intuition and how it can drive our choices.[45] Intuition can also help us appreciate our value as people and what we must bring to the table of life.[46] Manifesting the success that we desire has a starting point, and what better place to start than with ourselves?

What areas should we be observing in the quest of accepting ourselves and how we behave? Many factors can lead to achievement. Adolescence reveals some of the essential criteria driving success factors. Patrick Converse, Katrina Piccone, and Michael Tocci's research in adolescent behavior supposes that self-control and other positive and negative behaviors can determine how prosperous an individual will

---

44   Samuel Chand, *The Secret to Success: Three O's That Will Take You Anywhere in Life*. New Kensington, Pennsylvania: Whitaker House, 2020), 32-33, 42.

45   Ibid, 49-50.

46   Chand, 50.

be later in life.[47] The process of exhibiting conduct related to better self-control affects choices that may determine environmental elements that lead to better academic and financial outcomes.[48] The components that influence such decisions reveal extended concepts based on revealed behavioral patterns.

Self-control translates progress into success. Gareth Cook's review of research related to self-control predictors reflects the research of Psychologist Walter Mischel, who conducted a marshmallow test in 1972, testing the evidence of self-control among preschoolers.[49] The trial involved the simple choice of desire versus patience. Children were given a marshmallow and told to wait for some time before eating it and subsequently be rewarded with a second one.[50] The test revealed that the children had varying responses.[51] However, the results were more surprising years later and found those who had resisted the marshmallow as a child were performing better in life.[52] Past behaviors revealed patterns that predicted future outcomes. Understanding the past matters as it relates to where we are heading. It also offers an opportunity to self-correct. Based on the information research

47   Patrick D. Converse, Katrina A. Piccone, & Michael C. Tocci, "Childhood self-control, adolescent behavior, and career success." *Personality and individual differences*, 59 (2014): 66-67, 69.

48   Ibid, 69.

49   Gareth Cook. "Self-Control in Childhood Brings Future Success: Self-Control in Childhood Predicts Future Success." *The Boston Globe*. (2011), 1.

50   Ibid, 1.

51   Ibid.

52   Ibid.

provides, we can lead our children to make better choices by preparing them for accomplishment. Cook further suggests that preschoolers nationwide are being taught the skill of self-control through the 'Tools of the Mind' curriculum that teaches self-control and steers outcomes based on behavioral design.[53] Such research proposes that altering behaviors can affect achievement.

You may be thinking it is easier for preschoolers to make such changes. After all, they have not met the challenges that life has brought. And you may be correct. However, individuals with a desire to change can shift performance factors, no matter their age. Take the story of Lauri Vikmanis, a Cincinnati Bengals cheerleader. Vikmanis was not just any cheerleader.

> THE DRIVE TO SUCCEED ALTERS THE PROPENSITY TO CHANGE.

Vikmanis rooted her level of triumph in her discipline to succeed.[54] After many years in an abusive relationship, grueling practices, facing her fears of performance, and a limiting mindset, she changed her focus and pursued her dream.[55] As a result, she became a Cincinnati Bengals cheerleader at the astonishing age of 40.[56] The drive to succeed alters the propensity to change. The ability to succeed is also met by the challenge to keep going no matter what.

---

53   Cook, 2.

54   Laura Vikmanis, & Amy Sohn. *It's Not About the Pom-Poms: How a 40-year-old Mom Became the NFL's Oldest Cheerleader.* (New York: Random House, 2012), 184-188, 227-228.

55   Ibid, 98, 110, 115, 139-140, 227.

56   Vikmanis and Sohn, 194, 225-226.

> Each act of self-discipline strengthens every other act of self-discipline. Every act of persistence strengthens every other act of persistence. When you discipline your-self to persist, over and over, you like and respect yourself more and more. You become stronger and more confi-dent. Eventually you become unstoppable.[57]

What if you could change your trajectory based on under-standing your past and what makes you tick? What would you do differently today? How would that change your drive toward success? How would it define the way that you value yourself? The value you place upon yourself can affect your future. Perseverance can be a stepping stone to other positive behaviors.

What is Success to You?

Working toward a goal is only the beginning of the achieve-ment process. It is also essential to define what you want and why it matters. The idea of success as a driver of change could propose certain behaviors and detail their purpose. Just like the prize at the end of the race, success means different things for different people. In his research related to success, Zac Mclachlan notes that accomplishment establishes wealth for some while creating a legacy or opportunity defines achieve-ment for others.[58] Running a marathon might be the climax of a person's fitness journey, while it is a common practice

---

57   Tracy, 118.
58   Zak Mclachlan. "What is success." *Wainwright Star Edge*, Dec 04 (2020).

for others. Katie Peterson addresses victory in comparison to the construct of developing while researching the topic of success.[59] The idea is that poetry, like success, is about going somewhere and moving on a journey, not defined by any individual's idea of what it means to be true.[60] This logic proposes that a sonnet may take one's breath away while a simple 'Roses are red and violets are blue' would constitute the epitome of an influential poem for others.

In business and leadership, success ideas may define environmental factors and how others relate to workplace accomplishment. Promotions, bonuses, and acquiring the corner office may constitute success for some. For others, the idea of keeping a steady job, having a great work culture, or establishing brand recognition may be critical. The big picture reveals how you define accomplishment, even on an organizational level. Howard Schultz, CEO of Starbucks, delivered success in providing a feeling of Italian 'romance and community' in its coffee brand in the United States.[61] For Chick-fil-A, achievement rests in providing quality to consumers, according to US Business Review.[62] Don't let others define success for you. Determine what you want and why it means so much for you to obtain it.

---

59 Katie Peterson. "Success." *ASAP/Journal* 1, no. 3 (2016): 383.

60 Ibid, 383.

61 Howard Schultz, and Dori J. Yang. *Pour Your Heart into It: How Starbucks Built a Company One Cup at a Time.* (New York: Hachette Books, 1997), 53.

62 "Success done right; Chick-fil-A is one of the country's most success-ful quick-service chains, and it still focuses on quality food and community service", 2008, *US business review,* [Online], 9, no. 9 (2008): 173-174.

Identifying Obstacles

I have taken many road trips in my life. What I dreamed of most on those long stretches of the highway was uninhibited driving. If I get behind a slow car on the open road, I find a way to move ahead. Maybe you feel the same. However, driving on the interstate and driving in the city are two different things. Obstacles are bound to happen in the city, and perhaps more quickly than on a country road. In the city, you will find taxis, trolleys, and bikes, not to mention the other cars, buses, and trains. Reaching your goals means that you may have to face some hurdles. Things may not always function as planned. However, the ability to achieve does not always run smoothly. Perhaps you got a flat tire on the way to your child's dance recital, and you missed most of the show. Even though you may have arrived later than anticipated, let's keep things in perspective. The journey toward success may not always be perfect, but just like you arrived at the recital in time to witness the last performance, you can still make it through.

Nelson Mandela encountered many obstacles on his way to becoming a great leader. In his book, Nelson Mandela: A Bibliography, Peter Lamb shares how the South African leader watched his family experience the battle for land and witnessed his father's death when he was only a boy.[63] He struggled with the sense of entitlement other nationalities were afforded while the people in his land suffered from

---

63   Peter Limb. *Nelson Mandela: A Biography*, (Westport, Conn.: Green-wood, 2008), 5.

inequality.[64] Through it all, he became empowered to make a difference in his own life and the lives of others.[65] Sometimes, obstacles can become a catalyst for change. Embracing obstacles and using them as motivation can propel a person to become something different, something unbelievable. Do you recall that cheerleader Vikmanis from the Cincinnati Bengals and the obstacles she had to overcome? Becoming a cheerleader at 40 may not be easy, but if cheering is your lifelong dream, then the desire to excel is undeniable.

The Key to Opening Every Opportunity

Have you ever wondered why locksmiths exist? If I am locked out of my house or car, why don't I possess the same key I am paying others to maintain? Locksmiths are necessary. Locksmiths have mastered the art of opening locked items. While their existence may escape some, their artistry to perform at the required moment makes them an asset and a model for persistence in the face of adversity. Terry Trowbridge sums up the juxtaposition of their artistic impression in the following poem, "The Blind Locksmith," relating to the quandary associated with being able to uncover the more profound potential and frustrations associated with finding the right key:

For the blind locksmith
jigsaw puzzles are prayers.
His retirement is spent fingering little

---

64   Ibid, 7-8.
65   Ibid, 8.

quadrangle keys with teeth on all four sides.
Jigsaw puzzles turn his tabletop into
flat five-hundred-piece worlds made out of keys
freed from locks.

Five hundred keys that fit into each other.
A perfect plane of keys, properly fit
so that tumblers are superfluous.
The unseen picture is an inchoate tribute
to a lifetime of key cutting and lock setting.
The puzzle box sits on his knee
like five hundred rosary beads to enlighten him.

For the blind locksmith,
jigsaw puzzles are nightmares.
His dreams are filled with quadrangles that are
square locks with tumblers on all four sides.
He cannot read the box to know how boxboard
pieces will turn in his fingers, rotating left and right.
The nth frustration of a lifetime of skilled clicking,
he cannot remember if he held this one up to this
one already. After sorting, the edge pieces fence a
rectangular promise
of a world of locks that fit locks but shut no doors.
There are countless setbacks that he will have to
overcome.

The puzzle box sits open on his napping knee,
spelling a braille of uncertainty
over whether it is a bulwark against fading skills

or a bulwark against admitting the need for closure.[66]

What is the next step for someone poised to make changes in their life and move forward on the road to success? The answer to that question lies inside what I theorize as Master Key Thinking. This key works on practically every obstacle and every goal you set out to reach, much like the locksmith opening a puzzle box. Many people may seek this key their whole life, wondering why they cannot succeed, or they seek others' help to find it for them at a high cost. However, what if I told you that you already have the key? It is hidden in your house, and the only thing you need to do is open the unlocked box containing it. The box is *your mind.* The key is held deep inside your box. However, it is only a thought away. It is covered in intentions and surrounded by emotions. Using the tools in this book will clear away the things surrounding your **Master Key**. However, you must pick up the key and use it to gain access to other boxes filled with your potential, desires, dreams, and goals. The master key is simple, yet many people make it complicated. They avoid the process of picking up the key. They make excuses about why they cannot possibly hold it in their possession. They cover it up much like a dog burying a tasty bone, hoping that one day they will uncover it again in shock or surprise. Those who are viewed as successful quickly pick up the key while looking on in dismay at those who play ridiculous games shrouded

---

66   Terry Trowbridge. "The Blind Locksmith." *The Mathematical Intelligencer* 41, no. 4 (2019) 16.

in doubt and confusion and wonder why they cannot achieve results. The idea is to release the things that ail you and pick up your Master Key. For some, the key will require additional support to operate correctly. For others, it will be as simple as understanding how to place the key in the right location to open the box. What is this master key, you might ask? It is your **decision**.

> YOUR *DECISION* HOLDS THE ANSWER TO EVERYTHING THAT YOU WANT TO ACCOMPLISH.

Your decision holds the answer to everything that you want to accomplish. Your decision offers many facets that can lead you to the path of your dreams. Do you know why? Your decision, when appropriately wielded, is uninhibited. No one can control or possess it without your permission.[67] What drives your decision and how you employ that choice can support you in becoming the best version of yourself.

Some may argue that decisions are not always in our control. Joshua Shephard suggests decisions are the benefactor of several constraints that direct the path of the choices that an individual makes.[68] Logically speaking, some parts of this are correct. However, in the end, we are still in control of the decisions we make. Shepard further supports that the arbitrary thought processes that go against the grain also fall under our control, reflecting in our best interest when challenging those do not lead us to the results

---

67   Joshua Shepherd. "Deciding as Intentional Action: Control over Decisions", *Australasian Journal of Philosophy.* 93, no. 2 (2015): 335.

68   Ibid, 342.

we desire.[69] I like to think of this as deciding if you must, but only with trust. Ultimately, you know what you want to achieve. Initially, your achievement may not be clearly defined. However, your journey is a cautionary tale, prompting you to disengage from external factors that work against you arriving at your destination.

Feelings of fear may cloud your thinking and perhaps even challenge the way you feel about yourself. Understanding the source of anxiety can release much of the stagnation that holds you back from making the decisions you desire or need to make. In their book *Unhindered: Aligning the Story of your Heart,* Charity Byers and John Walker refer to such areas as 'sore spots,' blemishes deeply rooted in doubt, and hurts that filter the way people think.[70] They further suggest that releasing those thoughts to God frees us from the need to control everything in our environment.[71] Once we release control, we can begin to make decisions, understanding that we do not have to get things right every time. Movement can sometimes be more rewarding than getting it right. Remember that you are going somewhere, and that process comes with some elevated risks. I am naturally a very analytical person. As a result, people used to say to me, 'Don't get bogged down in the weeds.' I am challenging you to make a move to see and smell the roses in life.

---

69   Shepherd, 349.
70   Charity Byers, and John Walker. *Unhindered: Aligning the Story of Your Heart.* (Carol Stream: AVAIL, 2020), 104-105.
71   Ibid, 106.

When you are becoming all that you want, it can lead to scary thoughts. Part of the process of shifting your paradigm or way of thinking is to disassociate yourself from the things causing fear or doubt that can ultimately cloud your judgment. ***So, try this exercise. Close your eyes and imagine that you are at the top of Mount Everest.*** I know it is hard to imagine, and trust me, this exercise is going somewhere. Now, imagine you are at the highest skiing slope possible, and it's cold up there. The wind is at your back, and you are a little nervous. You have two options: you can ride the ski lift to the bottom or ski to the bottom. Now, closing your eyes again, imagine your choice and see yourself arriving safely at the base of the mountain and taking the small hike to your lodge to get a warm cup of hot cocoa. How is that cocoa? More importantly, no matter which way you choose to arrive at the bottom, the fact is that in your imagination, you arrived, correct? Some of you reading this got on a ski lift for the first time. For others, you got the thrill of a lifetime skiing down the slopes of Mt. Everest without leaving your cozy spot. This experience is the power of decision and how it creates additional paths for you. You must only free the clutter in your mental thinking enough to get to the next step.

Mental Moments: Where Do We Go from Here?

Now that you have visited the football field, the rose garden, and the mountain, think about where you would like to go next. Understanding the foundational vices that got you to this point in life can dramatically change your position when you allow yourself space and time to identify the items that can take you to your next role in life. Reflecting on the cultural examples, the choices you have made, and what you would like to do differently in the future creates a vast palette of ideas you can use as we delve further into becoming a successful mental mogul. Use the following questions as a framework to recap your journey thus far and prepare you for the next step in the process.

- What has your foundation taught you?
- What does success mean to you?
- Have you identified your obstacles?
- Are you ready to move forward with your key?

CHAPTER 3

GATHERING YOUR BELIEF

> 'Doubt is the only force capable of disturbing the seed or impression' ~ Neville Goddard.[72]

Believe. Achieve. Succeed. These words dominate many posters, t-shirts, bumper stickers, and blog posts. However, where does this logic originate? Can I achieve and succeed even if I am not the one doing most of the believing? What about the adage 'fake it until you make it'? Do the people who fake believing in themselves still get results? How exactly can I make myself believe when I am feeling the opposite?

A few years ago, I decided that I wanted a new house. I did not know how my husband and I would afford the type of home that I desired at the time. However, I just knew what I wanted, plain and simple. The fact is that we could afford the house that we wanted. We did not have a clear understanding of the disciplined behavior to save money at the time, or so we thought. My husband would pull up grand house plans all the time, and we would look over them, picking out the things that we desired the most. I liked the idea of having a large family room and indoor offices to have some space for

---

72   Neville, 100.

myself to dabble in music production without waking the whole house. Of course, my husband wanted the ultimate man space, which he later nicknamed the 'nerd cave.' With a college-age daughter living at home, I knew that she would also need a space to call her own. For two years, we looked at houses, visited models, and envisioned what we wanted. I even put the new home on a vision board, a poster-sized board full of pictures of the things I desired most. I began to see myself in a new home, though I had no idea where or when we would move. Suddenly and without expectation, a realtor tip sent me on a discovery drive to a new location. As soon as I visited the model home, I knew that we had found our new happy place, our new home. I wondered how this happened and how we went from seemingly little savings to precisely what we needed to purchase our new home.

Remembering my faith and understanding the revelation of Hebrews 11:1: 'Now faith is the substance of things hoped for, the evidence of things not seen' gave me the basis for understanding how we had arrived at this tremendous goal.[73] God had given me a clear framework for accomplishing my desires, and it began with a decision, followed by belief, and supported by action. The realization of an idea results from what we release into the atmosphere. God reminds us in Romans 4:17 that we should speak the visions we want to manifest into existence.[74] Penelope Russianoff champions this thought in a summary of discussing belief as to

---

73   Heb. 11:1 (New King James Version).
74   Roman 4:17 (Easy-to-Read Version).

the actual act of what we say.[75] She further supposes those words to be based on emotion.[76] Based on her discussion, the literal words we allow to filter into our brains create our beliefs. Jesus said that we should have child-like faith if we want to enter heaven and even praises those who possess that simplistic way of thinking.[77] Reminding ourselves not to overcomplicate thinking leaves room for God to step in and create beautiful realities in our lives.

In The Beginning

Where do the words we speak originate? We have creative genius living inside of us. How we choose to act affects those creative forces. Before we act, we must receive instruction. In the process of receiving instruction, destiny begins. In the book *The Tools: 5 Tools to Help You Find Courage, Creativity, and Willpower – and Inspire You to Live in Forward Motion*, Stuz and Michels suggested words come from the thoughts that come from a spiritual source, not from within ourselves.[78] To better understand this phenomenon, they discussed the power of living in gratitude for all that we have been given, from natural resources, such as the oxygen we breathe, to the way that our bodies function to support our lives.[79]

---

75   Penelope Russianoff. *When Am I going to Be Happy: How to Break the Emotional Habits that Make You Miserable*. (New York, New York: Bantam Books 1988), 44.

76   Ibid, 44.

77   Matt. 18:2-4 (NIV).

78   Phil Stuz, and Barry Michels. *The Tools: 5 Tools to Help You Find Courage, Creativity, and Willpower-and Inspire You to Live in Forward Motion*. (New York: Spriegel & Grau Trade Paperbacks, 2012), 155-156.

79   Ibid, 154-156.

Understanding how these criteria work in conjunction to support our physical existence helps us clarify how little we control. The fact is that I may think about breathing while I am awake. However, when I am asleep, something keeps me breathing correctly. Thankfully, it is a power greater than myself.

Positivity and rest go hand in hand. In their book *The Power of a Positive Teen*, Carol, Grace, and Joy Ladd reflect on the source of our well-being as good, providing the resources to combat powerful obstacles, lack of motivation, and burnout.[80] Stuz and Michels add to this idea of balancing gratefulness to remain connected to the source and neutralize negative thoughts that attempt to wreak havoc on one's mind.[81] Here is the problem with negativity. Just as the word negative supposes, it negates the things that the source says about us. God established us as people doing 'good works'.[82] According to Russianoff, living contrary to that reality allows other external forces to interject and place upon us what they feel to be right about our lives.[83] This way of thinking leads to other problems, such as rejection, because we no longer see ourselves in our balanced state, how the source sees us, and how God intended we live.

---

80   Carol, Ladd, Grace Ladd, and Joy Ladd. *The Power of a Positive Teen*. (New York: Howard Books, 2005), 19.

81   Stuz and Michels, 158.

82   Eph. 2:10 (NIV).

83   Russianoff, 51.

Getting Beyond Limitations

Embracing self-imposed or external limitations can lead to a series of actions that force us down the wrong path and further away from our box of potential and master key. Learning to identify the emotions that lead to negative thoughts can break the traumatizing effects they can have and allow us to understand and take account of our beliefs while valuing how we feel about ourselves.[84] Trusting in ourselves will enable us to put up a force field that keeps out intrusive thoughts and maintains a peaceful state of wellbeing.

The opposite of trusting in ourselves is worrying about what others think. Worry causes emotions related to a false sense of self-control.[85] While you assuredly have the power to decide what you want, your internal stasis allows you to relinquish control over matters that you cannot decide, such as the neighbor's carpet color. This thought may sound ridiculous. However, trying to control things that belong to others, like their personal thoughts, is futile. Focus on yourself and choose to set your thermostat in life. In his delivery of leadership theories, Peter Northouse supposes that internal development constitutes the ability to make changes that can affect potential, stamina, and growth.[86] You have a better chance of seeing a situation through by focusing on the skills that allow you to set the benchmark for how you will react.

---

84   Russianoff, 65.

85   Stuz and Michels, 150.

86   Peter G. Northouse. *Leadership: Theory and practice.* (Thousand Oaks, CA: SAGE Publications, 2004, 50-51).

Bridging Positive Thoughts With Self-Worth

The ability to focus on what makes us unique can create opportunities for others to see the same in us. Robert Igor learned the importance of understanding his worth and value and controlling his thought process through gratitude in the face of disappointment.[87] He desired greatness for himself; however, before achieving the position that one would dream of, he had to take a side step, filling the role of second in charge at ABC Television.[88] Understanding how to control his emotions led him to become President of ABC Entertainment.[89] He ultimately went on to become CEO of the Walt Disney Company.[90] Keeping emotions in check can lead to big payoffs. According to Eric Weber, self-belief becomes appreciative when you know that you have the right qualities for a job.[91] Profiting from affirming emotions based on personal beliefs is the icing on the cake for those who choose to believe in the value of themselves.

Surrounding Emotions with Positive Environments

Amicable emotions can lead to better choices. Relationships can prove to be significantly affected by the feelings that we demonstrate with others. Relationships also act as

---

87   Robert Iger. *The Ride of a Lifetime: Lessons Learned From 15 Years as CEO of the Walt Disney Company.* (New York: Random House, 2019), 32.

88   Ibid, 30-32.

89   Ibid, 33-35.

90   Ibid, 110.

91   Eric T. Weber. "Self-Respect and a Sense of Positive Power: On Protection, Self-Affirmation, and Harm in the Charge of "Acting White"." *The Journal of Speculative Philosophy* 30, no. 1 (2016): 49-50.

incubators, much like Petri dishes in a lab. David Walton suggests that relationships reveal communication and ideals related to trust.[92] Feelings associated with mistrust breed behaviors that compound negative emotions and lead to misalignments based on frayed thoughts and misunderstandings.[93] Understanding the source of emotions can relieve pressure because it gives individuals another perspective from which to view situations.[94] Being married for over two decades has helped me understand that I do not know everything about relationships.

I have discovered that even in a close relationship, it is important to recognize the value in myself first and in others. When I value my house plants, I choose to give them water and food. Removing the dead weight from plants, giving them the care they need, and providing water allows them to reach their full potential, according to suggestions by Anad Arium.[95] When I give my plants what they need, they grow, much like people. In his book *The Fred Factor*, Mark Sanborn explores the idea that relationships are only as good as the amount of time spent making them function optimally.[96] After so many years of marriage, I often get the things I want. However, there are times when I do not. In those moments, I remember that I do not have to require everything all the

---

92   David Walton. *Emotional intelligence: A practical guide.* (New York, New York: MJF Books, 2012), 101.

93   Walton, 101-102.

94   Ibid, 102.

95   Anand Airun. "Prepare Plants to Soak in Nourishment during Rains: Happy GARDENING." *DNA (Mumbai, India)* (2016).

96   Mark Sanborn. *The Fred Factor.* (New York: Currency, 2004), 43.

time. 'The steady pace wins the race' is a motto that I use to remind myself that nourishment takes time. Walton further encourages that providing nutrition at the correct moment supplements the balance of emotions.[97] Understanding that relationships are important leads to the discovery that they affect other parts of our lives based on how well the people inside are balanced and value others.[98] The initial question as it relates to sustenance is, who are you feeding? Hopefully, you are feeding yourself first. The next question is, what are you feeding yourself?

Positivity is Refreshing

I have a skeptical side. When it comes to icy roads, I trust no one. Historically, ice and snow have not been my best friends. I remember leaning on an experienced driver to take the wheel of my car during a blizzard once, and we became stuck in a snowbank. A more experienced driver came along and helped us to get dislodged. While I usually enjoy the first snowfall of the season, I am challenged by how others wield their vehicles down the highways' slippery slopes in my city. In my mind, a couple of snowy days, followed by some balmy temperatures, prove the perfect scenario for this Southern-born girl. Perhaps my skepticism developed after spending a couple of winters in Illinois and New Jersey. Walking with snow up to my knees is not my idea of fun. I am more of an iced tea on the sun porch or cozy blanket at the football game kind of person. It is in this area that I find

---

97   Walton, 57.
98   Ibid, 11-12.

a challenge. I want snow, not the icy roads that come with it. How do I cope with the juxtaposition of the two scenarios? I celebrate the snow, and I tolerate the ice with a positive attitude. I do not propose that you put up with things that are detrimental to your spirit. I am merely encouraging you to embrace the benefits of thinking positively, which is one of many tools that we will explore on your journey to formulating success. Snowfall brings snowmen and snow angels, and both bring me joy. An anticipated emotional state of joy helps me overlook the less-than-desirable parts of winter.

Finding joy in the things that surround you gives you positive positional power. The tremendous biblical prophet Nehemiah reminds us of the power of joy in Nehemiah 8:10:

Nehemiah said, 'Go and enjoy choice food and sweet drinks, and send some to those who have nothing prepared. This day is holy to our Lord. Do not grieve, for the joy of the LORD is your strength.' (Nehemiah 8:10, NIV).[99]

When I want to give up or look at the wrong side of things, going back to my source allows me to reboot, much like a computer, and work out the kinks. Establishing gratefulness lightens the load, according to Ladd et al.[100] Such appreciation resets my path and allows me to see things with greater clarity and through a renewed posture. In the book *Grace, Not Perfection: Embracing Simplicity, Celebrating Joy*, Emily Ley supports positively pouring into yourself, which enables

---

99   Neh. 8:10 (NIV).
100 Ladd et al., 112.

your faith to strengthen and worries to dissipate.[101] Ladd et al. further support the thought of focusing on others which can also develop a sense of happiness reflected in our own lives.[102] The art of balance constitutes changes in the constructs that encourage your thoughts.

Positive Environments Move People

Surrounding yourself with the right environment can cause major shifts in your thinking. Such theories are supported by researchers Tracy Epton et al., explore behavioral effects using the example of health-related circumstances that use positive affirmations to change how people respond regarding the choices they make in life.[103] This logic could suppose that the answer to what ails the less-than-positive side of life can be corrected by substituting positive reinforcements. Each day, I start with a Bible verse, followed by meditation and prayer. Sometimes, I just lay in bed and think about nothing, allowing my imagination to wonder about journeys that I have never experienced, like life on the moon or what I will make at my next family cookout. Some of my most significant plans, songs, and inventive ideas have come from these moments where I give my mind space and time to wander without interference. I know that some people like to wake up to the latest music tunes or the morning news. Sometimes, interjecting your thoughts before others get

---

101   Emily Ley. *Grace Not Perfection: Embracing Simplicity, Celebrating Joy.* (Nashville: Thomas Nelson, 2016), 29.

102   Ladd et al., 112).

103   Tracy Epton et al. "The Impact of Self-Affirmation on Health-Behavior Change: A Meta-Analysis." *Health Psychology* 34, no. 3 (2015): 193-194.

a chance to impose theirs gives you the ability to access creative areas you may have never dreamed of before. It is also in the free mind space that we can interject nourishing thoughts that can yield powerful results and create a foundation upon which we can grow and flourish. Weeds choke out healthy plants. Inserting positivity reflects the plant food that we need to make things grow. One way to insert plant food is through the practice of positive affirmation.

Integrity Choices

Growing ourselves leads to a stable posture and allows us to make sound decisions. Making appropriate decisions is one of the supportive tools for using the Master Key. Ladd et al. suppose the thought that integrity is displayed on the outside yet grown on the inside.[104] Thoughts and actions reveal our character reflected in the basis of truthfulness.[105] Becoming a person of integrity that is grounded in substance synchronizes the ability to stand unapologetic before others. Northouse supposes leadership as opportunities that simulate individuals transferring their positions of influence and knowledge to others.[106] Supposing leadership is something that you desire in life; focusing on the inside creates a balanced substance that can stand the test of time. Of course, the opposite would have drab potential and lead to institutions lacking the ability to effectively change others' lives, as supported by Kendra Momon in her book *Being as*

---

104   Ladd et al., 88.
105   Ibid, 89.
106   Northouse, 2004, 3.

Leading.[107] Croker, Niiya, and Mischowski provide further context to suggest that focusing on affirming values affects caring for others.[108] The choices that you make today produce mental vices that can affect the future of others.

Positive affirmations add richness to the language that we feed ourselves. They allow us to choose the words that move us and supplement our self-talk with inspiring messages that can carry us throughout the day. Epton et al. encourage affirming yourself which means reflecting on values that can modify behaviors toward actions that provide positive reactions.[109] Think about the last positive affirmation that you told yourself. If you cannot think of any, it's time to develop some. Your positive declarations may be as elaborate as reciting an entire message, a family saying, or a simple mantra such as: 'You have got this' or 'You can do this.' No matter where you start, choose something that moves you and gets you going even when you don't want to move. Remember, when you use the Master Key, it incites movement, even if it means taking the ski lift to the mountain's bottom. These determinants are not to be confused with the type of inflation that presumes the imposter syndrome. Kirstie McAllum supposes that the imposter syndrome reflects a generation stiffened by the desire to create an imbalanced

---

107   Kendra Momon. *Being as Leading: Your Roadmap to Shaping Culture Through Life's Disruptions.* (Sanford, Florida: AVAIL, 2020), 91.

108   Jennifer Crocker, Yu Niiya, and Dominik Mischkowski. 2008. "Why does Writing about Important Values Reduce Defensiveness? Self-Affirmation and the Role of Positive Other-Directed Feelings." *Psychological Science* 19, no. 7 (2008): 746).

109   Epton et al., 188.

state of being based on unrealistic inflation of abilities resulting from overindulgence from their parents during their adolescent years.[110] She further proposes creating scenarios where students can work independently of educators to build self-esteem and achievement.[111] Reflecting on the skill of bragging, a healthy dose of realism reflects descriptions based on positive reassurance that propels versus narcissistic behaviors that leave people feeling turned off.

Mental Moments: Where Do We Go from Here?

Believing in yourself means taking steps to uncover the thought processes that may be hindering your progress. Sometimes, this is related to how we speak to ourselves, how we use our emotions, or how we treat others. It is essential to understand what makes up our daily language, as it has the power to affect how we view and accept ourselves. The balance of self-worth is vital as it guides the choices that we make when interacting with others. Building the daily habits needed to either change our self-talk or build upon our strengths is formed in the day-to-day decisions we make. We can crowd our minds with what others think or give ourselves the space to grow and develop our creative thoughts. Using the foundational steps you are building, let's begin to explore the framework upon which you can start incorporating your choice of paths from a decision to

---

110 Kirstie McAllum. "Managing Imposter Syndrome among the "Trophy Kids": Creating Teaching Practices that Develop Independence in Millennial Students." *Communication Education* 65, no. 3 (2016): 364.

111 Ibid, 364.

results. We will also explore theories that encourage success factors based on environmental concepts related to building a mental support system for leaders. The action steps revealed will help support the necessary changes needed to positively develop your daily life and personal journey. The following questions will help you reflect and provide a continuous collection from which to grow.

- What are you saying to yourself daily?
- Are you moving beyond any limitations toward your best self?
- Are you nourishing yourself and others?
- Is your attitude in balance with your posture?
- Have you built healthy affirmations into your self-talk?

CHAPTER 4

GOAL-SETTING FRAMEWORK

Most people do not walk around with the idea of achieving leadership success at the forefront of their thinking. Perhaps we want to win in life or want to have a nice home and success within our chosen fields. However, for many desiring high levels of accomplishment, success results from meeting the challenge of proficiently leading others. Most of what has driven this book expands the desire to determine how business leaders can become more successful in life, in an easier manner. My personal experiences foster the idea that leadership success can be somewhat foreign to the everyday individual. Finding a path to more extraordinary accomplishment takes a back seat to waking up, driving to work, and sitting at a desk for eight hours. When grounded in a plethora of sometimes seemingly productive actions, the repetitive experiences may lead some down the path of mediocrity, which is a less-than-desirable goal when scaling achievements. I formulated most of my experiences with leadership based on my entrepreneurial successes. Others may have developed the concepts within the conduits of organizations owned by others. Using the examples of those around me to establish guidelines, I have a better understanding of how people relate to products and each other in self-owned organizations, such as developing positive experiences around direct customer contact. I have also found success within corporate structures by focusing on achieving personal development while seeking ways to create and nurture relationships with internal clients and team members that support community growth and development.

Developing others is a crucial step for organizations hoping to achieve goals and meet objectives. Of course, there are many approaches to understanding theory related to organizations and design, as supported by Gareth Morgan in his book *Images of Organizations*.[112] The concepts support multiple positions that offer understanding spread across the myriad of successful businesses in the market. Richard Daft also supposes the development phase of organizations as a conduit of how they function to fully maximize strategic results that substantiate success.[113] The process of successful development starts with creating meaningful results at the individual level and developing an environment that encourages change at every organization's level, as expressed in organizational charts.[114] Such diagrams are the tangible expression of how the company functions daily.[115] On the surface layer, the general chart acts as a grid for the flow of processes. Beyond the level of such an approach are the individual constituents that make the work happen. Those

---

112   Gareth Morgan. *Images of Organization.* (Thousand Oaks, California: She Publications, 2006), 5.

113   Richard Daft. *Organization Theory & Design* (12 ed.). (Boston: Massachusetts, 2016), 87.

114   Ibid, 88.

115   Daft, 89.

individuals perform to expand the contingencies that make the company function at an optimal level.[116] Breaking down those processes further focuses on the tasks that impact the organization's success.[117] The visible factors depicted within an organization remain mostly hidden from view. However, much like the results of faith and belief, there is an excellent benefit to visualizing effects or processes. In the book *Strategic Thinking and the New Science*, T. Irene Sanders discusses the benefits of interpreting non-linear processes through visualization based on researcher Edward Lorenz's approach of displaying non-linear computations in visual forms.[118] Such constructs allow the moving parts to come to life during constant changes. Lorenz's concepts led to chaos theory approaches, and the *Lorenz Attractor* was used to depict the behaviors behind non-linear mathematical processes.[119] As a result, such factors make it easier to characterize visual effects related to an organization's behavioral aspects. Basically, this model reflects chaos in a tangible form, which is non-constant and can be used to reflect the same in organizational behavior.

Organizational fit is another factor common to establishments. According to Daft, the fit within an organization formulates an individual's ability to reference internal components provided to affect the identified core or guiding

---

116   Ibid, 119.
117   Ibid, 142.
118   T. Irene Sanders. *Strategic Thinking and the New Science: Planning in the Midst of Chaos, Complexity, and Change* (New York, New York, 1998), 58-59.
119   Ibid, 59-60.

principles within a company.[120] It is important to note that these core principles are in flux, and the individuals assuming the roles may change in status as it relates to organizational fit.[121] Such changes mean leveraging commitments to sustain individual, team, and corporate growth as one cohesive unit for the organization. As a collective part of my research, several individual components for leader success within organizational units have populated diverse yet supportive constructs for creating a nurturing environment for growth. **The resulting concept that bridges such articles is founded on the *LeaderMind* theory.**[122] The approach introduces a rich and strategic process that combines the elements that promote leader success in organizations. It combines the principles of skills-based functions to interpret individual input and organizational support.[123] The *LeaderMind* theory manifests a visual model that partners with constituents in the hope of achieving personal goals through a formulated plan across the backdrop of organizational leadership development.

120   Daft, 126.
121   Daft, 127.
122   Coley, 2020.
123   Ibid, 2020.

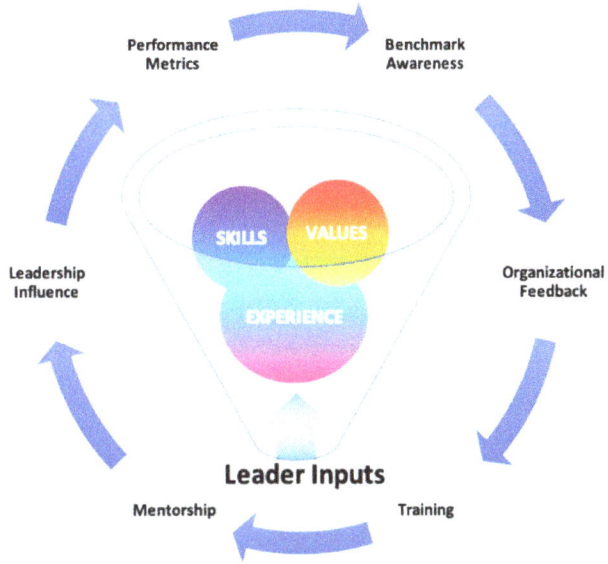

Figure 4-1 Leadermind Theory

Earlier research summarizes the thoughts related to the theory of *LeaderMind*:

> The *LeaderMind* leadership development plan utilizes benchmarks and a potential leader's skills and value assessment combined with the organization's influence to develop and promote growth in leaders desiring to perform within the global context. The strategic plan utilizes six areas of influence to create a platform for leadership development: values and skills assessments, benchmark awareness, training initiatives, mentorship from senior management, global experience opportunities, and performance metrics.[124]

---

124   Coley, 2020.

Much like *mind mapping* (See Chapter One), the *LeaderMind* theory utilizes inputs that create proposed outputs. Based on the constructs of the idea, the platforms of skills, values, and experience operate best when combined with practical organizational components to release optimal outlays in an individual and equip them with the fortitude to accomplish big goals.[125] The idea of such a framework can be transposed outside of the leadership arena and used effectively to help others achieve success in their everyday lives. Individuals can use behavioral actions coupled with a useful framework to meet desired goals and function to assist with continual mental focus.[126] The words that make up the theory title, *LeaderMind*, are fused to remind those in leadership that mental focus is synonymous with effective leadership strategies. The next few chapters will address the *LeaderMind* pillars of Mentorship, Training, Influence, and Performance outcomes related to success achievement, combined with the effects of values and experience as mental inputs that initiate change in an individual's behavior. The *LeaderMind* theory further proposes that combining desired activities related to building mental fortitude with the inputs of the *LeaderMind* paradigms work to better assist individuals in overcoming obstacles that lead to success.

---

125   Ibid.
126   Ibid.

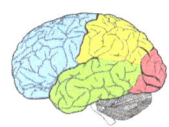  

| Mental Fortitude | LeaderMind Theory | Successful Outcome |

Figure 4-2 Influence of Mental Fortiude on Leadermind Theory

Mental Fortitude

Exactly what is mental fortitude? Why is it essential in regard to success? How we get along in life is dependent upon many factors. According to Vanessa Meyer, mental focus based on behavioral design can teach concepts that help individuals encompass tremendous feats.[127] Learned behaviors create expected and predictable results in real-life experiences exhibited through exercising mental muscles.[128] Individuals can use the practice of positive imagery to create successful outcomes. Learning how to approach the exercises can provide opportunities for implementing ways to achieve goals, even in the face of difficult situations. Mental fortitude builds the muscles associated with achievement by using external factors to strengthen subsequent scenarios.[129] Just as in physical exercise, individuals can develop mental aptitude over time, as supported by Kouzes and Posner in

---

127   Vanessa M. Meyer. 2018. "Sport Psychology for the Soldier Athlete: A Paradigm Shift." *Military Medicine* 183, no. 7-8 (2018): e272.

128   Ibid, e272.

129   Ibid, e275-e276.

their book *The Leadership Challenge*.[130] The collaboration between mental fortitude and supportive behaviors assists individuals when formulating a plan for sustained mental growth.

How to Perform in Balance

You are not perfect, and neither am I. I remember trying to be the best student in elementary school. I would always show up for my third-grade class on time and do my best to listen to the teacher. I would sit quietly in class and be friendly to all the other students. However, no matter how hard I tried, I was never considered the teacher's favorite in my mind. Though my grades were good, and I excelled at benchmark tests, I still remember getting paddled in the third grade because my desk was messy, and my teacher had asked me to clean it several times. There were many issues with this scenario. First, I had no framework to use in organizing my desk. I remember looking at the desks of the other students and wondering how they could maintain such organization. I also thought that my worth was connected to how much the teacher or others liked me. This thinking was a fallacy that took years to overcome. My organizational issues were finally addressed during my military service, though I admit that clutter can become a friend from time to time. My issues related to pleasing people is an ongoing struggle. However, I remember that the only one that I truly must please is

---

130   James Kouzes and Barry Posner. *The Leadership Challenge: How to Make Extraordinary Things Happen in Organizations* (5th ed.) (San Francisco, California: The Leadership Challenge, 2012), 208.

God, and that settles any thoughts of unworthiness because, fortunately, He accepts me as I am.

'Jesus wept.' (John 11:35, NIV)[131]

Whether you think displaying emotions is good or bad, most see a crying leader as one that either has a heart or has no backbone. Thinking of the former is vital to the goal of success. To think that even Jesus cried before His followers leaves room to consider humanistic needs as drivers for balance. According to Joseph Badaracco in his book *Defining Moments*, the philosopher Plato assumed that perfect constructs depicted the reality of how people function in their minds.[132] However, his student Aristotle understood that people operate in balance based on their senses' influences.[133] Thinking of this balanced emotional life where we live in stasis with emotions is much like the analogy of correct back posture and the satisfaction that it can deliver. No one wants to walk around bent over all day. However, it is important to bend over from time to time, even if you are only tying your shoes. The range of emotions addressed in the personal evaluation of success fallacies may remind individuals of everything going wrong in life. However, embracing emotional development as an asset can help us experience life in a more expressive way. Make this a reason to strive for

---

131   John 11:35 (NIV).
132   Joseph L. Badaracco. *Defining Moments: When Managers Must Choose Between Right and Right.* (Boston, Massachusetts: Harvard Business School Press, 1997), 43.
133   Ibid, 43.

success and change your future trajectory while embracing yourself.

Performance Matters

Why begin with the discussion of performance? After all, performance concepts appear near the end of the *Leader-Mind* theory cycle. With any good storyline, starting at the end allows the proceeding inputs to align with the desired outcome. When individuals think of how they might perform, the taste of the last meal they cooked, a work presentation from last week, or their gym workout, it may leave some discerning room for growth. According to Kevin Moore, the fact of the matter is that we are in a constant state of flux and full growth for those who expect it, requiring promotion to achieve something in life that sets them apart from others.[134] Life is complicated, and expectancies can become clouded. The quest for achievement can push individuals to focus more on the finish line and less on the voyage. We are always on a journey to some future destination.

The path to the desired destination can become tiresome and laden with the quest to finish at all costs. Some may grow weary and think that rest is never truly an option until we leave this earth. When such emotion overcomes our thoughts, God encourages us to rest in His arms of support instead of relying on ourselves: 'Come to me, all you who are weary and burdened, and I will give you rest.'[135] We must remain open

---

134   Kevin Moore. *Wellbeing and Aspirational Culture*. (Cham: Springer International Publishing AG, 2019), 33.

135   Matt. 11:28 (NIV).

to the fact that we need help daily, especially as it relates to personal development and the interjection of supportive performance breaks to assess progress. No individual has ever built a large bridge on their own without understanding that there may be hiccups along the way, additional hands may be needed in the construction, and the satisfaction may come more from the journey (building) than the destination (completed project). We are human and supportive performance is randomly necessary.

Ley further reminds us of the concept of grace used to fulfill our desires.[136] It is in the arms of God's grace that we find solace in knowing that it is great to reach for more but okay to fail sometimes.[137] It is the place of rest that we can utilize in the process of the journey. Why is this important? According to Kouzes and Posner, failing means that there is room for expansion and growth and that we will reach the pinnacle of success in each area if we give ourselves the space for change and the correct mindset to keep pushing forward.[138] Developing the right mindset embraces an understanding that perfection is not an attainable level of achievement unless you earn a perfect score on a video game, and even then, you might leave with a sore bottom or thumbs from hours of playtime. The possibility of a sore bum should leave you with the thought that there is another way to measure performance. Ley further addresses grace as the achievement of joy and embracing our fallacies in a

---

136   Ley, 8.
137   Ibid, 9-10.
138   Kouzes and Posner, 208.

way that allows us to love ourselves and others.[139] Love is the beginning of all that is important in life. Without love, we are doomed to fail without any room for recompense. 'Love bears all things, believes all things, hopes all things, endures all things.'[140] Remember the power of love, even in reaching your goals.

The concept of love circles back to Yuill and Little's discussion regarding Maslow's Hierarchy of Needs and the desire to achieve self-actualization, to make a difference, and to aspire to more for ourselves and others, ultimately to be successful.[141] Achieving success requires a realization that there are factors beyond self. Giving others of ourselves creates a path of existence that supersedes that of merely reaching a personal goal and defines an altruistic leader's giving nature, as supposed by Fallen Mallén et al.[142] At the end of our journey, we should hope that we have expended every ounce of who we are based on personal desires into others' lives, thereby giving them something to use and pass on in their circle of influence. Salas-Vallina, Andres, and Joaquin Alegre suppose the more altruistic an individual's mindset, the more likely they are to positively affect others and influence engagement and satisfaction.[143] Operating

---

139   Ley, 12, 14, 94-95.

140   1 Cor. 13:7 (English Standard Version).

141   Yuill and Little, 264.

142   Fermin Mallén et al. "Are Altruistic Leaders Worthy? the Role of Organizational Learning Capability." *International Journal of Manpower* 36, no.3 (2015): 273.

143   Salas-Vallina, Andres and Joaquin Alegre. "Unselfish Leaders? Understanding the Role of Altruistic Leadership and Organizational

from a perfectionist mindset may close us to the potential that our worthiness depends on more than our ability to get it right. Sometimes, getting it wrong can also teach valuable lessons and lead to great returns.

> THE PROCESS OF *GIVING* IN THE DEVELOPMENT OF MINDSET AND PURPOSE PULL AT THE STRINGS OF ONE'S HEART AND SETS THE SUCCESSFUL APART FROM THE UNSUCCESSFUL.

How can we love others when we don't love ourselves? There are some fundamental principles that outlay performance and the standards we should use to achieve such initiatives. Whether we are operating in service to ourselves or others, we must first remember to put ourselves in the shoes of others. As a reflection of business success, Mary Kay Ash, founder of Mary Kay Cosmetics, reminded us that a company could be built upon the Golden Rule's principles and treating others with dignity, respect, and love.[144] The ability to do for others as we would do for ourselves means that we must first treat ourselves well. This expression of love determines the overall framework to achieve success. Lorin Woolfe addresses the giving nature of successful businesses such as Ben and Jerry's in their quest to give back to their communities as a precept for success.[145] The process of giving in the development of mindset and purpose pull at the strings of

Learning on Happiness at Work (HAW)." *Leadership & Organization Development Journal* 39, no. 5 (2018): 636.

144 Mary K. Ash. *Mary Kay Ash: Miracles Happen.* (3rd ed.) (New York: New York: Harper Perennial, 1994), 168.

145 Lorin Woolfe. *Leadership Secrets From the Bible: From Moses to Matthew: Management Lessons for Contemporary Leaders.* (New York: MJF Books Fine Communications, 2002), 53-54, 56.

one's heart and sets successful individuals apart. Giving sets us free to be more successful in the eyes of God.[146] It allows us to consume more than success or failure or unabridged commitments. Understanding how to give to others creates space for other things to grow, such as our determination to make things happen, no matter what.

Influence Me Please

Focusing on mental aptitude requires addressing the support pillars that can initiate change. The first of many changes depends on the individual standing next to you. Many have never thought of this individual as someone who can aid or hinder the process. With strategic direction, choosing the right support can provide both stability and accountability. In his book *The Making of a Leader: Recognizing Lessons and Stages of Leadership Development*, Robert Clinton depicts the idea that individuals leading the charge do so based on the experience qualities associated with their personal growth.[147] They learn to understand themselves and the values that reflect personal growth.[148] Progression is crucial, and revelation can provide the opportunity to uncover hidden obstacles often missed when we are operating blindly.[149] The supportive environment portrays a cycle of extended processes passing between individuals to formulate shared learning. Using

---

146   Ibid, 144.
147   J. Robert Clinton. *The Making of a Leader: Recognizing the Lessons and Stages of Leadership Development* (Colorado Springs: Colorado: NavPress, 1988), 166.
148   Ibid, 171.
149   Ibid, 171.

a personal growth tool expressed through leadership can serve as an expanded path to a clearer vision on the road toward success.

Getting in the Know

Developing others would seem to constitute placing something inside of them to formulate more success. In the book *Why Winners Win: What it Takes to be Successful in Business and Life*, Gary Pittard shares that individuals in the learning process must first identify a need, followed by an activity that produces results.[150] To successfully implement the training process, organizations must know what their individuals need. This method requires understanding the individual and their culture to implement change factors based on successfully constructing values. For example, suppose the organization exists as a collective, where the group's interest supersedes the individual. According to research by Li-Yeah Lee and Chia-Ying Li, such a scenario is best supported by training suited toward the individual's fit within the culture's framework to induce commitment and better performance.[151] The skills developed should be functional at the level of their design within the organization. Much like gardening and fertilizing plants, development

---

150 Gary Pittard. *Why Winners Win: What It Takes to Be Successful in Business and Life*. (Milton, QLD: John Wiley & Sons, Inc., 2016), 63.

151 Li-Yueh Lee and Chia-Ying Li. "The Moderating Effects of Teaching Method, Learning Style and Cross-Cultural Differences on the Relationship between Expatriate Training and Training Effectiveness." *International Journal of Human Resource Management* 19, no. 4 (2008): 604.

training assumes that individuals will function better within their roles based on their full growth potential realized over time.

The Gentle Giant of Change

Move over developers; there is a new construction worker in town to assist with developing others. The mentor is an individual's change advocator. Mentors ultimately have the task of working themselves out of a job. According to Shirley Peddy in her book *The Art of Mentoring: Lead, Follow and Get Out of The Way*, a mentor's goal is to assist individuals with gaining the wisdom needed to meet objectives.[152] Many people may use social media influencers or famous stars as mentors; however, I challenge you to move beyond surface-level direction and seek the assistance of those who can demonstrate through example and challenge you to do the same.[153] Utilizing the path of mentorship can create significant changes for organizations.

Mental Moments: Where Do We Go from Here?

When embarking on the road to change, mindset can either assist or hinder the process. Those seeking to develop a better strategy for change must focus on the criteria used to establish support and a strong starting point for achievement. The interactions between mental fortitude and behavioral actions provide a better understanding of growth inside and

---

152   Shirley R. Peddy. *The Art of Mentoring: Lead, Follow and Get out of the Way* (2nd ed.) (Houston, Texas: Bullion Books: 2001), 2.

153   Ibid, 3-4.

outside organizational constructs. You can use the following questions to ensure that you are entering the personal development and goal achievement arena with the appropriate posture:

- Are your goals based on perfection or grace?
- Outside of yourself, who are you serving?
- Are you working with focus?
- Is your performance attitude in alignment with your focus?
- Are you gearing up to build a supportive network to meet your goals?

CHAPTER 5

TOOLKIT ONE –
HABITS, SKILLS, FOCUS

> 'You know why I like tools? Because they fix things—you tear down a motor, see the problem, it's right there— boom; it's fixed. I wish I could fix things between us that easily.' ~Tim Taylor: Home Improvement, Season One.[154]

My husband's company invests in many tools. In addition to these purchases, my husband also had to buy his own tools when he started as a field engineer several years ago. I could not understand why we had to spend hundreds of dollars before he had even received his first paycheck. He reminded me that without the right tools, workers could not get the job done.

Work requires workers, and those workers require tools to complete processes. According to Ellen Shell in her book *The Job: Work and its Future in a Time of Radical Change*, a growing number of companies are moving toward automation in situations where machines are more equipped to outperform people.[155] Just think about the last time you

---

154 Quote Catalog. 2021. https://quotecatalog.com/quote/peter-tolan-you-know-why-i-8abVdja.

155 Ellen R. Shell. *The Job: Work and its Future in a Time of Radical Change.* (New York: Currency, 2018), 78.

paid a bill via telephone. Did you talk to a live person or a machine first? The introduction of Artificial Intelligence replicates human behavior tendencies through software use, according to research by Stephen Tansey.[156] Automation does offer several benefits for economic growth. According to Shell, the manufacturing process provides a creative opportunity for workers to wield their knowledge and induce innovation on a larger scale.[157] Mechanization also reduces human capital costs and relies on technological advancement to increase productivity.[158] As a result, the minuscule idiosyncrasies that produce change may be affected by the support networks that assist specific work processes. By 2030, analysts predict digital manufacturing will begin to replace traditional practices.[159] The skills needed to perform such functions and promote stability will function based on what workers know and their ability to successfully deploy that information as a profitable skill in future markets.[160] Tools are an effective support network that can aid workers in skills-building for performance.

Investing in workers is essential. In their book *Business Model Generation: A Handbook for Visionaries, Game Changers and Challengers*, Alexander Osterwalder and Yves Pignuer suppose the idea that companies need people to reach

---

156 Stephen D. Tansey. *Business, Information Technology and Society.* (New York, New York: Routledge, 2003), 29.

157 Shell, 272.

158 Ibid, 273.

159 Ibid, 287.

160 Ibid, 287-288.

goals.[161] The centritistic view of placing emphasis on workers is further supported by Samuel Chand and Cecil Murphy in their book, *Who's Holding Your Ladder: Leadership's Most Critical Decision – Selecting Your Leaders,* placing emphasis on the individuals that lead operations and their need for optimal support staff to achieve objectives.[162] Tansey further supposes that the information required to perform processes is not limited to machines.[163] People are an important part of the business process. According to Daft, the precepts associated with caring for people mean that companies take the time to invest in their greatest commodity with the required ideals and techniques.[164] The example that organizations set determines the perception of leadership when it comes to taking care of people. In the Bible, Jesus took the time to invest in His disciples through training.[165] He took the initiative to make sure that they had everything needed to do their jobs well.[166] Pushing the envelope within organizations depends on effective constituent preparation. In his book *The Light Prize: Perspectives on Christian Innovation,* Gary Oster supports the idea regarding innovative competencies which are induced via training that further provides the knowledge

---

161   Alexander Osterwalder and Yves Pigneur. *Business Model Generation: A Handbook for Visionaries, Game Changers, and Challengers.* (Hoboken, New Jersey: John Wiley & Sons, Inc., 2010), 35.

162   Samuel Chand and Cecil Murphy. *Who's Holding Your Ladder: Leadership's Most Critical Decision - Selecting Your Leaders.* (Niles, Illinois: Mall Publishing Company, 2003), 3.

163   Tansey, 9.

164   Daft, 399.

165   Matt. 10:1-15 (NIV).

166   Luke 9:1-27 (NIV).

that people need to succeed now and in the future.[167] Experience and knowledge push the envelope when it comes to the preparation that meets opportunity.

Based on this new knowledge initiative, workers will need support to develop areas requiring additional reinforcement to move into the next technological area. The *LeaderMind* theory supports the prescription of tool kits that individuals can utilize to support success's behavioral functions. Several tools assist the *LeaderMind* theory framework. The next two chapters cover six supportive tools: positive habits, skills building, focus, self-care, guidance, and constructive correction.

✗ Tool One: Positive Habits

I start each day with prayer, meditation, and a Bible verse. I have been working on this habit for years. I remember when I first started this behavior. I would use the app on my phone to set reminders to perform this task. However, I would sometimes fall off track and go weeks without remembering to read my morning Bible verse. Of course, I blamed this on businesses, sleepiness, and everything that hindered me from remembering to take the time to center myself. I noticed that things seemed to run smoothly on the mornings when I took the time to meditate and pray. However, when I forgot or tried to squeeze this time into the five minutes before the workday began, my mornings were flustered with non-productive activities and scenarios. Once I began to take

---

167   Gary W. Oster. *The Light Prize: Perspectives on Christian Innovation.* (Virginia Beach, Virginia: Positive Signs Media, 2011), 65.

notice, I changed my routine and no longer needed reminders to set aside the time in the morning before I got out of bed to take care of one of the most beneficial behaviors that I have discovered.

Habits Based on Behavior

Teachers get the bulk of the work when it comes to formulating lasting behavior. Teachers are with the children that they service for much of the day. They are witness to many forms of student behavior, positive and negative. When addressing less-than-desirable behavior, it is crucial to understand why it started or why it continues to occur.[168] Analyzing behavior depends on discovering the underlying feelings associated with the expressed behavior.[169] A key to building positive action is instituting reinforcements that would influence the repetition of the desirable outcomes.[170] In the example regarding meditation and prayer, the underlying emotion and feeling was a desire for calmness in my day. The positive reinforcements helped me to attain the tranquility needed to function at work properly.

Negative reinforcements also promote performance. However, research dictates that there may be unexpected side effects that promote additional behavioral issues, primarily when used to adjust adolescent behaviors.[171] The negative

---

168   Lisa Rodgers. *Building Positive Momentum for Positive Behavior in Young Children: Strategies for Success in School and Beyond.* (London: Jessica Kingsley Publishers, 2018), 15.

169   Ibid, 15.

170   Ibid, 16.

171   Ibid, 17.

rewards provoke fear and further feelings that children may relate to misunderstanding and doubt.[172] Such structures, including disciplinary actions, should be used to replace processes that lead to better judgment over time.[173] The use of reinforcements adds to or detracts from desired behaviors. I remember getting home from school one day before my parents arrived. They had been out running errands, and the time had slipped away. During those days, it was safe to let kids off the bus without seeing their parents. At the time, I was eight years old. I went to my home and sat on the steps of the front door. After approximately 15 minutes, the sun began to beam down on the concrete steps where I sat. It felt as though I had been there for hours, though I knew that my parents would be home soon. However, the thought of relaxing inside my home, where it was cool, tempted me to do the unthinkable. I found an open window and made my way into our house. Minutes later, my parents arrived home. Surprised when they questioned how I had made it inside our home, I described how hot it was outside and that my older brother had opened the door for me. The fallacy with this story: my brother was still at school in football practice. Of course, my parents punished me for entering through the window and lying, which led me to make better choices in the future.

The repeated behaviors that we display reflect the habits that we form. Those habits lead to positive or negative outcomes. In the Bible, Joseph was the wealthy and most

---

172   Rodgers, 17.

173   Ibid, 17.

favored son of Jacob.[174] Joseph was a dreamer, and his enthusiasm led him to prematurely release his God-given dream to others who did not value his position in his father's eyes.[175] In his book *Running with the Giants*, John Maxwell reflects on Joseph's enthusiasm to share his dream with others.[176] As a result, Joseph encountered many detrimental consequences based on others' feelings.[177] However, he learned from his behavior and later formed habits that would save his family and his nation.[178] [179] Maxwell also supposes that conveying practices that reinforce positive behaviors assist with appropriately using the toolkits. Additionally, according to Rodgers, praise improves positive behavior by 80 percent.[180] We must strengthen the actions that we would like to witness in others consistently.

⚒ Tool Two: Skill-Building

I learned how to type without formal instruction. I can type quickly and proficiently; however, I do not use the traditional methods that many of my counterparts use. I notice that I touch the keys differently, and I often look down at the keyboard versus the screen. However, I have built this skill and many others over time in my way. Skill-building

---

174 Gen 37:1-4 (NIV).

175 Gen. 37:5-10 (NIV).

176 John C. Maxwell. *Running with the Giants: What Old Testament Heroes Want You to Know About Life and Leadership.* (California: Warner Books, 2002), 28.

177 Ibid, 28.

178 Gen. 45:4-7 (NIV).

179 Maxwell, 31-34.

180 Rodgers, 39.

goes hand in hand with habits. According to Robert Clinton, skills are assumed over time and require submission to the process.[181] In the book *Creative Engagement in Occupation: Building Professional Skills*, Margaret Coffey, Nancy Lamport, and Gayle Hersch address the posture that occupational therapists utilize in reinforcing rehabilitative skills to produce results in patients.[182] The rehabilitation process allows participants to express themselves in the therapist's presence and beyond.[183] Over time, the repair leads to restoration and the increased ability to improve performance.

Skills-based workers in the mid-range of pay utilize common techniques, while those receiving higher pay utilize specialized processes.[184] Due to the increase in mechanization, those with specialized skills are discovering diminished working roles in their usual sectors, forcing them to seek lower-skilled positions not affected by the increase in mechanistic functions.[185] However, higher skill levels are associated with satisfied workers based on securing jobs with greater financial rewards.[186] Additionally, higher skill aptitude increases the expectation of work environments and the work that they perform.[187] Individuals who acquire additional

181   Clinton, 81.

182   Margaret Coffey, Nancy Lamport, and Gayle Hersch. *Creative Engagement in Occupation: Building Professional Skills*. Slack Incorporated,2015.), Chap. 2.

183   Ibid, Chap 2.

184   Ibid.

185   Ibid.

186   Ibid.

187   Ibid.

education and invest in skill-building can also secure employment more readily.[188] This status suggests that building skills is a positive attribute when functioning in work roles.

The first time that I gave a sales presentation, I sold $200. For me, this was a large amount of money. As a new business owner, I had invested close to $3,000 in products, business supplies, and training materials. It would be several months before I held my first presentation, which yielded over $500. I would eventually go on to develop the skills required to reach higher sales levels over time. There were several deals in the interim that yielded nothing in terms of financial gain. Perhaps you have been reluctant to invest in your personal skills development. I encourage you to look at the investment as an expenditure that can yield great rewards. If you plan to work at anything, you may as well position yourself to reap as many bonuses as possible.

⚒ Tool Three: Focus

The discussion of focus requires attention toward a direction. When I focus on academics, I am working towards a stated goal, hopefully one that includes a high grade. I intensely perform my work with an end goal in mind. Without direction, we are shooting arrows in the dark, aimlessly placing our attention on things that may not matter in the grand scheme. God instills purpose in our lives. Without meaning, we do not need tools, processes, mental aptitude, or success. We would walk the blundered path of life, going from one

---

188 Ibid.

moment to the next without cause. Unfortunately, I suppose there are individuals who live with the plan, 'let me make it to the next five minutes.' God said that He has given us hope in a future that can bring great reward: 'For I know the plans I have for you,' declares the Lord, 'plans to prosper you and not to harm you, plans to give you hope and a future.'[189]

Why would God give us hope if He did not intend for us to have focus? Focus is a skill that takes time to develop. Kids usually focus on having fun, ice cream trucks, cartoons, and recess, all concepts with limited focus. There is nothing wrong with these things from the perspective of adolescence. However, to see the success that we may desire as adults, a devotion to discovering our purpose and directing our actions toward our goals may require more than 15 minutes of our time.

Rick Warren describes our purpose as bringing delight and glory to God.[190] He further discusses the human plight to suffer, wondering if it is essential to seeking others' approval for the life choices we make.[191] When we know why we exist, it relieves many of the pressures associated with pleasing others or trying to figure out what we should be doing.[192] We gain a full understanding of our designed purpose when we act out the true meaning of our creation and embrace God as the giver of that purpose.[193] Once you have discovered your purpose, you might wonder how you should focus your actions.

---

189   Jer. 29:11 (NIV).

190   Warren, 63.

191   Ibid, 29-30.

192   Ibid, 30-31.

193   Ibid, 20-21.

Directing Focus Toward Others

Actions are a matter of assigning a behavior toward a result. When it comes to the behaviors related to focus, they should be utilized in service to others.[194] The act of mental focus further determines how to serve others.[195] Simply allowing God to work through us to support others places us in the act of service. Great leaders like Martin Luther King, Jr. and Abraham Lincoln had humanistic faults. However, they were synonymous as great servant leaders because they looked beyond their present conditions to take a risk to improve others' lives. I want to think that this was out of a response to serve God by serving others. God is everywhere and encompasses our entire lives. Understanding that God's presence is at work in us and others helps direct and decipher any altruistic behaviors related to helping others. According to Gene Veith, Jr., in his book *God at Work: Your Christian Vocation in All of Life*, we can also work to better understand that God cares about the world's state and reigns over it.[196] He demonstrates the care and concern that He wants us to show others. We may not have national platforms or influence; however, we live among others in our communities. If you look to the person on your left and right, you may find that they need your God-given purpose today.

---

194   Ibid, 257.
195   Ibid.
196   Gene E. Veith Jr. *God at Work: Your Christian Vocation in All of Life*. (Wheaton, Illinois: Crossway, 2002), 26.

Mental Moments: Where Do We Go from Here?

Using the tools in our toolkits allows us to acclimate to the processes that can increase mental fortitude and induce behavioral changes. As you understand these tools and how they can help you achieve success, the mental shifts gained should help you begin associating these factors to bridge any gaps and reinforce the areas that need support. You can use the following question to strengthen the benefits of using your tools to support personal success:

- Have you identified behaviors that no longer serve you?
- What habits are you forming to support your success?
- Are you investing in your skillset to determine future growth?
- Have you discovered your purpose?
- Are you working with a focus on serving others?

CHAPTER 6

TOOLKIT TWO - SELF-CARE, GUIDANCE, CORRECTION

The first three tools of positive habits, skill-building, and focus direct consideration toward external contingencies. The following three tools attend to the internal concepts that affect success behaviors. Balance precludes concentrating on the external over the internal. The hope is that the tools presented bring better balance to success behaviors as a functional part of acquiring achievement.

Tool Four: Self-Care

Self-Care Saturdays seem to be the buzzword in my circle of friends and family. People are taking their private time more seriously in my community. Their dedication to their care rituals is an excellent example for someone like me. I will admit, of all the tools, this one has taken me the longest to embrace. As a mother and wife, I tend to place my concerns on the back burner and focus more on supporting the roles of those around me. Embracing my academics caused me to shift this focus. I pursued my education as a personal quest. Therefore, ensuring that I completed the task became a vital function in my life. As a result, there were quite a few weekends that we ordered out, or I folded the clothes a little later than usual. Of course, there were also the moments when I chose to lay in bed all day because I was utterly exhausted. However, I have learned over time that setting aside personal time is extremely important. If I do not take care of myself, who will? I must exist in wholeness to have a life and relationship with others. Taking care of self takes on a whole new meaning with maturity and the demands of life.

Daphne de Marneffe discusses the role of mothers in her book *Maternal Desire: On Children, Love, and the Inner Life.* She supposes that new mothers often operate in conflict when choosing between the career that they love and feelings of guilt when taking care of or spending extra time with their children.[197] I am sure that there are several fathers in this situation as well. Parents need a holiday to reset themselves for the continued task of childrearing. I spent many years as a young mother in the Navy attempting to balance time between work and home. Some days seemed longer than others, and active-duty life came with the challenge of ensuring military commitments progressed when duty called. Living overseas away from family complicated the situation at times. Due to the high career demands, I built my support network with friends who I would call to help when I became overwhelmed. I am still grateful for these women today. They were not family members, far from it. They were women serving abroad like me, some as military spouses, others as active-duty military mothers. I

---

197   Daphne de Marneffe. *Maternal Desire: On Children, Love, and the Inner Life.* (New York, New York: Time Warner Books, 2004), 52-53.

am thankful for their selflessness and ability to offer help to a young mother in need of respite.

Take Care of Self to Serve Others

Taking care of yourself is not selfish. Christina M Godfrey et al. postulate self-care and the reflection of therapeutic attention that people receive and self-preservation for its preventative measures.[198] Self-care can use formal or informal protocols and fluctuate in definition based on professions.[199] Understanding how to incorporate self-care can mean the difference between wellness and sickness in terms of its effectiveness at preventing the latter with the inclusion of supportive social constructs.[200] Things will get busy in life from time to time. Stressors can build up as we complete daily functions. Steven Stein addresses the stressors that can also cause issues in other life areas, mostly avoidable by reducing their effects through proper care in his book *The EQ Leader: Sharing Passion, Creating Shared Goals and Building Meaningful Organizations through Emotional Intelligence*.[201] We must take the time to recharge so that we do not falter when required to perform. In her book *Look Great Feel Great: 12 Keys to Enjoying a Healthy Life Now*, Joyce Meyer quotes

---

198   Christina M. Godfrey et al. 2011. "Care of Self – Care by Other – Care of Other: The Meaning of Self-Care from Research, Practice, Policy and Industry Perspectives." *International Journal of Evidence-Based Healthcare* 9, no. 1 (2011): 4.

199   Ibid, 4.

200   Ibid, 6, 9.

201   Steven J. Stein. *The EQ Leader: Instilling Passion, Creating Shared Goals, and Building Meaningful Organizations through Emotional Intelligence*. (New York: Wiley, 2017), 62.

'common sense' as a key to achieving balance.[202] Taking care of ourselves is a biblical mandate, as reflected in 1 Corinthians 6:19-20:

> Do you not know that your bodies are temples of the Holy Spirit, who is in you, whom you have received from God? You are not your own; you were bought at a price. Therefore honor God with your bodies.[203]

The principles surrounding balance are essential to achieving success. Meyer further shares that distractions can occur that derail us from the goals we are trying to accomplish when we allow situations to prevent us from giving our best.[204] Reflecting on my years as a young mother reminded me of the importance of taking care of myself as a precursor to effectively pouring into others' lives.

✗ Tool Five: Guidance

Guidance helps us stay on track when pursuing a role or path toward our goal. According to Meyer, sometimes individuals want to do things on their own, especially if they do not comprehend the purpose of why they are completing an action.[205] Making the most of a situation is determined by ensuring effective results.

---

202   Joyce Meyer. *Look Great Feel Great: 12 Keys to Enjoying a Healthy Life Now.* (New York, New York: Time Warner Book Group, 2006), 77.
203   1 Cor. 6:19-20 (NIV).
204   Meyer, 2006, ix.
205   Meyer, 2006, 77.

Skill-building, positive habits, and training are great tools; however, we must know how to use this information to be proficient at what we do. Additionally, a key factor to success recalls the correct way to apply all the knowledge and information we absorb. Organizations should set up their leaders for success. Developing others should include the assurance that they know where they are going, what it takes to get there, and whether they are on track to arrive at their destination according to the prescribed plan.

Have you ever forgotten how to get to a specific store or restaurant? You may have visited the location several times in the past. However, situations may seem a little fuzzy, or at least enough to make you turn on your navigation system to avoid getting lost. You have a vehicle, gas, and excellent driving conditions. Yet, it would be best if you still had assistance to get to your destination. According to Peddy, guidance from others works to assist with the process and ensure that we have objective support when reaching for a goal.[206] It took me three Thanksgiving dinners before I felt comfortable cooking a turkey without a family member's assistance. Even though I had written instructions, the support reassured me that I would deliver a juicy entrée to the dinner table for the holidays instead of a dry bird. In his book *The Art of Startup Fundraising: Pitching Investors, Negotiating the Deal and Everything Else Entrepreneurs Need to Know*, Alejandro Cremades shares the idea that companies in the startup phase of their business often rely on others'

---

206   Peddy, 87.

guidance to assist with making the right decisions that promote success.[207] The addition of varying environmental conditions precludes that assistance would be welcomed, especially by novice entities.

Acting alone can cause issues related to a lack of knowledge, skill, or how to use the two. Either way, Gary Collins claims the result of trying to meet objectives without support often fails as revealed in his book *Christian Coaching, Helping Others Turn Potential into Reality.*[208] We need the help of others to succeed, starting with God.[209] God reminds us in the second book of Corinthians that He has everything that we need to succeed:

> But he said to me, "My grace is sufficient for you, for my power is made perfect in weakness." Therefore I will boast all the more gladly about my weaknesses, so that Christ's power may rest on me.[210]

When acting, we must rely on God if we want to prosper. The culmination of efforts needed to succeed may come from a variety of sources. Just remember that the primary source feeds all the other ones.

---

207   Alejandro Cremades. *The Art of Startup Fundraising: Pitching Investors, Negotiating the Deal, and Everything Else Entrepreneurs Need to Know.* (Hoboken, New Jersey: John Wiley & Sons, Inc., 2016), 23.

208   Gary R. Collins. *Christian Coaching: Helping Others Turn Potential into Reality.* (Colorado Springs: Colorado: NavPress, 2002), 204-205.

209   Ibid, 205.

210   2 Cor. 12:9 (NIV).

✕ Tool Six: Correction

Strategic processes are everywhere. People are usually telling or describing to others how to do something and how to get somewhere. You may hear things such as: 'Get on the 4 a.m. train when going to the city to beat the traffic,' or 'Historically, the reports will be late on Friday; therefore, ask your team to complete them on Thursday.' However, what happens when things do not go as planned? Correction can function as a tool. However, adjustment utilizes two significant substructures to be effective: reflection and accepting constructive criticism.

Reflection Reveals Truth

Think back to a time when you were trying to accomplish something, and you could not achieve your goal. Sometimes, reflection reveals a past that we may desire to hide. A great example involves retesting. Perhaps taking a test over might provide a higher score. Retesting might be critical for those taking an aptitude exam to gain entry to areas such as the military, law school, or medical programs. In these situations, it's all about strategy. So, how do we effectively reflect and correct?

Looking at what you offer requires keen insight. Robert Clinton reminds us that we cannot become so busy that we do not allow the time to determine our status as a crucial step in the beginning process of development.[211] To move forward, you must be able to access your unique talents and abilities. Beyond such insight, you must be honest about areas where

---

211   Clinton, 155-156.

you may need assistance. Usually, leaders self-report at a higher level based on their perception.[212] However, when external data meets personal perception, individuals gain a more realistic picture of their abilities.[213] For those gaining entrance into programs, establishing tests may serve as benchmarks for proficiency levels. For those functioning in work environments, performance metrics may measure these roles. However, if you're attempting to be the first person to launch a career that no one has ever heard of, utilizing your peers' input to access your growth status may assist in the process.

Decide to Build

Instructors have a unique responsibility to ensure their students achieve success in the classroom. In an authentic learning environment, Arnie Bianco proposes in his book *One-Minute Disciple: Classroom Management Strategies that Work*, how students are encouraged to engage in the learning process through an appraisal that provides an advantageous experience.[214] The feedback received should support the intended outcomes desired. Less-than-desirable actions, achievements, or scenarios that reflect subpar performance within the organizational environment can cause some to become entrapped by focusing on others' motives. There are situations where people may tend to be more abrasive versus constructive when providing feedback, such as in the medical

---

212   Ibid, 63.
213   Ibid, 63.
214   Arnie Bianco. *One-Minute Discipline: Classroom Management Strategies that Work*. (San Francisco, CA: Jossey-Bass, 2002), 40.

field, as shared by Jennifer Percival (2015) in the *Nursing Standard Journal*.[215] Albeit, the need for a more intense approach may mean the difference in a life saved in a medical environment, comments that leave you feeling encouraged to achieve better support efforts versus those that leave you feeling unmotivated to make changes. If the information you receive regarding performance is helpful, move forward with the determination to learn something from others. Focusing on the working areas and how you can strengthen them removes the negative connotations associated with highlighting fallacies.[216] The process of learning takes precedence instead of focusing on your mistakes.[217] Collins further supposes that the best way to respond when you make a mistake is to admit that it occurred, remit to those that it may have affected, rectify actions, and progress forward.[218] Gaining a clear perspective ensures that progression can occur with fewer obstacles. During the analysis process, ask questions of others to garner possible solutions.[219] Learning to appreciate productive feedback will allow you to embrace perspectives and focus on improvements.

---

215   Jennifer Percival. "Constructive Feedback." *Nursing Standard* 20 no. 28 (2006): 72.
216   Ibid, 72.
217   Ibid, 72.
218   Collins, 232.
219   Collins, 320.

Assessing Tool Valuation

'If the only tool that you use is a hammer, you treat everything like a nail.' (Bianco, 2002, 72).[220] Some tools will be more effective than others when gaining the support needed in your quest for success.[221] You will need to take a proper assessment of the tools that are most important to you. Use the ones that you are naturally accustomed to and build upon the others when needed. When you are ready for the next task, ask yourself whether you have accessed all the tools available to you.

Mental Moments: Where Do We Go from Here?

Sometimes, we need small reminders that we have access to a plethora of ideas and networks. Look to your community or circle of friends for additional support. Perhaps there are workshops in your area or online that can assist with tool development. Within organizations, you may wish to make suggestions regarding the training you need to develop as a leader. Also, remember to aid others when needed in support of their work. Boats go faster when multiple people are rowing in the same direction. The following questions can assist with accessing the remaining tools in your toolkit:

- Do you dedicate time to taking care of yourself?
- Is guidance a part of your learning process?
- Have you assessed your current skillset?
- Do you accept and implement constructive feedback?
- Are you using the right tool for the task at hand?

---

220   Bianco, 72.
221   Ibid, 72.

CHAPTER 7

SUCCESS BUILDING RESULTS

The *LeaderMind* theory encompasses several aspects associated with behavioral practices that support meeting success objectives. Mental fortitude plays a significant role in achievement, as reflected in exploring social and behavioral constructs. This chapter details the research process to test the *LeaderMind* theory and portrays useful outlays.

In his book *The Practice of Social Research*, Eric Babble shares that working in the research field can reveal outcomes related to understanding how people operate in their environment.[222] Understanding the patterns associated with similar behavior helps us to determine the results through observing those behaviors in individuals.[223] The researcher developed the purpose of testing the *LeaderMind* concepts to answer the critical question reflected through this book: which behaviors foster success and subsequently impact goal achievement?

Using Field Research to Test Behaviors

The Success Behaviors Research covers critical strategic leadership practices based on qualitative research used to test the behavioral aspects of the *LeaderMind* theory. The

---

222 Earl Babbie. The Practice of Social Research. (Belmont: California, 2004), 7, 17.
223 Babbie, 7.

study used methods associated with human-social research initiatives. It involved a framework that induced an environment where the researcher could observe social behaviors through a series of interviews. Mentoring participants reflect and summarize the conduct of professional business mentees desiring the opportunity to meet personal goals in addition to their own.

The research protocols explained in this chapter combine the efforts of understanding the behaviors that affect success and identify the mindset of leaders as an example for those aspiring to achieve. The Success Behaviors Project's research used descriptive observation to determine behaviors and activities that have a positive effect on participant success. The goal of the activities reflects examples that individuals might see in a working organization environment. This research designated vital concepts to help individuals and organizations understand the representation of the *Leader-Mind* theory through visual attributes. The hope is that you will be able to use the information gained throughout this process to further understand how to apply the concepts to develop your success. Keep in mind that the research was used as a pilot to test the protocols over three weeks. Supplementary research may be needed to test additional conventions such as cultural influences and participant motivation. Additionally, duplication of the processes may not constitute the same results as those expressed in the research.

The Testing Process

The Success Behaviors Research included 15 participants working within the framework of a simulated environment, providing relevant data. The groups comprised critical players in the pilot, business professional, and business mentor groups. Each group had a significant role in developing the research process based on their descriptive attributes. Each group contributed pertinent data based on behavioral research to help garner a consensus on the *LeaderMind* theory's behavioral aspects.

The Pilot Group

The pilot group tested the outer limits of the *LeaderMind* theory: behavior choices, mentor inputs, training, and feedback (Coley, 2020). The process of using business professionals working in corporate environments ensured that the individuals came from similar career backgrounds. The *LeaderMind* theory addresses the process of identifying the choices most related to achieving success for individuals who desire a commitment to change. Focusing on a smaller group allowed better control of the subjects' processes and useful research through managed interviews that did not heavily impose upon their regular functions.

The Business Professional Group

The professional business group included sole proprietors owning one or more businesses. Their role provided instructional guidance and role modeling indicative of successful organizations. The professionals also provided formalized training and instruction based on success objectives and their personal experience. Individuals from this group were selected because they own at least one business and have experience leading others. The business professionals also offered systemic support based on the simulated organizational environment that provides training and the 'lead by example' approach.

The Business Mentor Group

The third group of participants functioned in dual roles, providing guidance and ensuring support for the individual in the pilot group through one-on-one conversations. The business mentors ensured the pilot group established action steps to achieve short-term goals within the research period successfully. The business mentors have all worked in various capacities, leading, guiding, and mentoring others in a corporate setting. They were given minimum suggestions, such as active listening tips and recommended meeting times. The business professionals supported the structured framework of the *LeaderMind* theory by addressing the pillars related to training and mentorship. Additionally, the business members simulated the positive aspects of sound middle management represented in an organization with a balanced cultural structure.

Researching the Behaviors

For three weeks, the Success Behaviors Research observed approaches that reviewed the pilot group's behaviors and the founding principles of the business professionals and mentors. The research also observed the interaction between the pilot group subjects and the business mentors. The study gathered information based on a series of interviews to collect data from the various research groups. Research groups were small to develop and mimic the intimacy of relational aspects involved in one-on-one training within organizations. The pilot group included six participants, with a corresponding number of business mentors. The business professionals represent the senior leadership found in many organizations. The professional business group included three individuals, all successfully operating businesses delivering products and services in various markets across the United States. The research simulated individuals' responses within an organization's scope, though the practices also apply to individuals outside of a formal entity's constructs.

Establishing a Timeframe

Have you ever driven somewhere and wondered how you got there? You were sure that you put the keys in the ignition of your car. Somewhere between your starting point and your destination, your mind began to wonder, and then, voila! You arrived with no recollection of turning your vehicle or using signals along the way. Understanding that timeliness matters when people are developing new habits, the *Leader-Mind* theory sought to address supportive measures that would benefit those involved in the research processes. In their book *Do Business Better: Traits Habits and Actions to Help You Succeed*, Damian Mason and Larry Winget reference the role of habits as purposeful contributors to the effects of success over time.[224] You must desire the process of forming new habits. When you are intentional about a habit, it becomes routine as your subconscious takes over the approach.[225] Establishing new routines are critical to becoming successful.

Breaking the Routine

The *LeaderMind* theory introduced the pilot group to new activities. The pilot group participants were encouraged to instill positive daily behaviors such as utilizing encouraging videos, podcasts, and literature. They assessed their skills and reflected on the areas where they could improve. The group also attended weekly training sessions to introduce them to successful leaders in the community. Each pilot group participant was randomly assigned a business mentor and met weekly to discuss their short-term goals for the research timeline. The business mentors also offered insight into the participant's goals and aspirations, tips, and strategies to succeed, and productive feedback based on their performance each week. The process introduced multiple strategic steps to achieve success in a short period. Breaking routines mean that you sometimes must deviate from your comfort zone and become creative. Achieving success also relies on a strategic process that moves you away from comfort or business as usual.

---

224 Damian Mason and Larry Winget. *Do Business Better: Traits, Habits, and Actions to Help You Succeed.* (Newark, New Jersey: John Wiley & Sons, Inc., 2019), 62.

225 Ibid, 62.

The Success Behaviors Research results proposed a variety of choices regarding the observable aspects of the *LeaderMind* theory. Based on the implications, the research could address actions related to an individual's inputs based on their skills, values, and experiences concerning the pillars of leadership, mentorship, training, and feedback. The reflection with the business mentors provided an additional layer of observation in conjunction with self-assessment related to individual benchmarks represented by identified goals.

Leader Inputs

The *LeaderMind* theory relies on input skills for success. The participants' skills reflected a myriad of choices based on individual input. The information assessed offered insight regarding the inputs relative to unique gifts, values, and experiences. As indicated in Figure 7-1, the pilot group demonstrated research skills as dominant leader input traits.

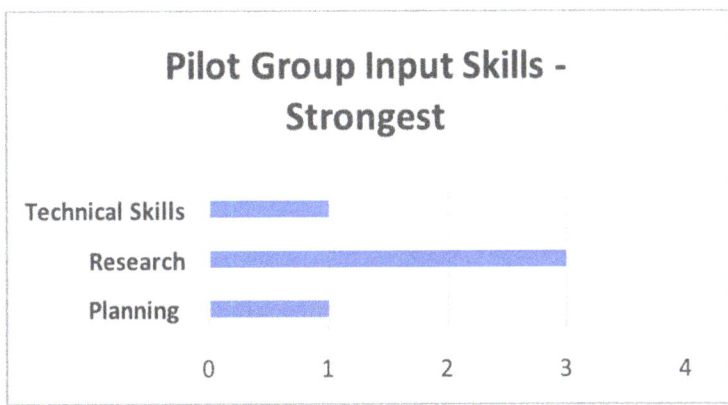

Figure 7-1 Pilot Group Input Skills - Strongest

The research process focused on developing individual skills. The researcher also asked the pilot group to identify their most significant areas of concern (time management) related to their beginning skill sets to balance perspective. The observation assessed the skills they wished to improve concerning their daily lives, as indicated in Figures 7-2. Similar constructive assessments could help organizations identify areas of weakness within an organization to better develop leaders and support self-identified weaknesses.

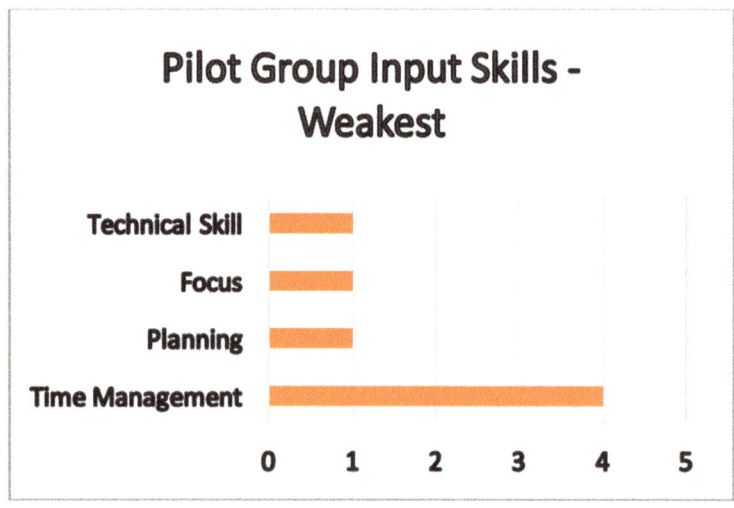

Figure 7-2 Pilot Group Input Skills – Weakest

Perception plays a vital role in how people think. The values associated with the research used indicators related to how the pilot group participants perceived the definition of success. The information provides valuable insight when focusing on emerging leaders' ideas, as reflected in Figure 7-3, with most participants defining success attributes in relation to goal attainment. How do you perceive success in your own life? Think about success as it relates to your performance on the job when handling money. How might your actions shift if your definition of success changed? If your definition of success was attaining the top role in your company, how would you behave tomorrow at work? Perceptions, like or not, matter. Developing a healthy mindset when it comes to success outcomes can define your behavior and ultimately your achievements.[226] Focusing on the foundational processes such as success beliefs can lead to positive outcomes in several organizational areas.

Figure 7-3 Success Definition – Pilot Group

LeaderMind Pillars

The *LeaderMind* theory addresses vital components related to supporting pillars addressed throughout the Success

---

226   Paula Caligiuri. *Cultural Agility: Building a Pipeline of Successful Global Professionals.* (San Franciso: California: Jossey-Bass, 2012) 51-52.

Behaviors Research. The resulting outputs convey implications of managing the internal components of the structured process. The research supports the developed processes used to determine the behaviors addressed because of participant observation and reflection indicated throughout the surveillance of success constructs.

Role Modeling

The pilot group participants determined the impact that mentorship had on their ability to assess their performance, define goals, and achieve success. Figure 7-4 reflects the role of mentorship during the research process. Considering the impact of mentorship and coaching, the roles and attributes of leadership development are contingent upon successful role models and their ability to convey new concepts for participant adoption.

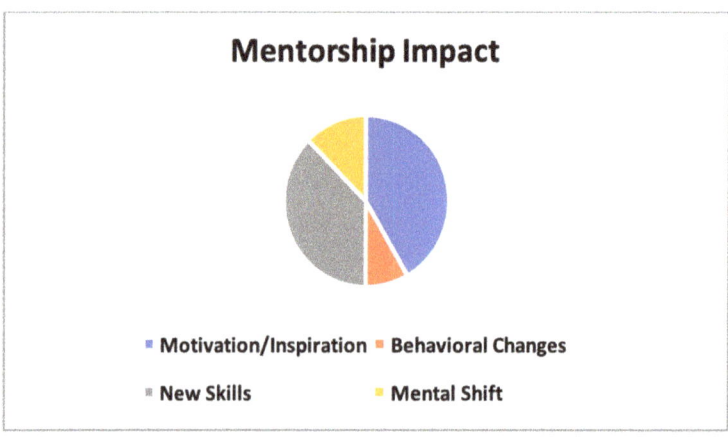

Figure 7-4 Mentorship Impact on Pilot Group

Training and Leader Influence

Education, whether formal or informal, offers the ability to support training and encourages skill development. The participants' results also reflected responses concerning leader influence and interactive training sessions with the business professionals. The participants' responses covered areas such as directed focus, inspiration, and increased knowledge regarding business practices as outputs of their participation in the weekly sessions. Figure 7-5 reflects the observed responses.

Figure 7-5 Leader/Training Impact On Pilot Group

Performance Metrics

The Success Behaviors Research also addressed the impact of goal-setting and its relationship to achievement within a specified time frame. This focused effort supported the measured goal-centered actions by setting a benchmark for participant outcomes. Pilot group participants highlighted the results of their short-term goals as reflected in Figure 7-6.

Figure 7-6 Goal Status – Pilot Group

Research Feedback

Participants reflected upon the impact that the Success Behaviors Research and their improvements addressed through self-observation. Table 7-7 reflects the effects of the Success Behaviors Research on the pilot group participants related to their overall behavior. The overall impact reflects the most changes in areas associated with seeking or acquiring new knowledge about the pilot group participants' goals. Actions related to planning, such as creating new plans and developing new technical skills that could assist with the development, were also noted.

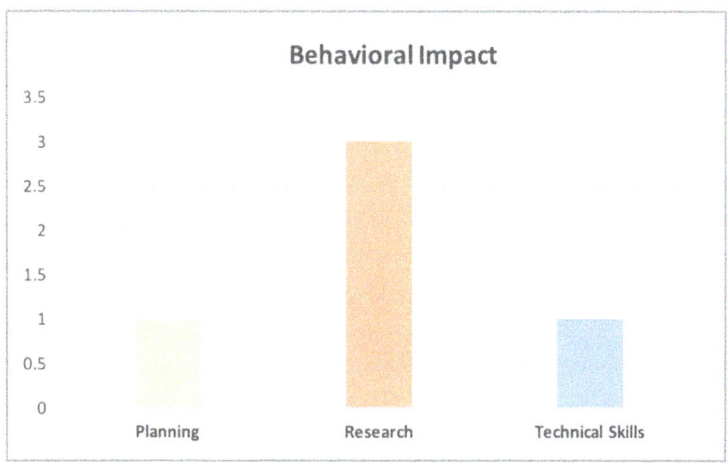

Figure 7-7 Behavioral Impact On Pilot Group

Research Outcomes

By the end of the Success Behaviors Research, the pilot group participants reassessed their skills and identified the areas of improvement resulting from the protocols. The following chart (Figure 7-8) displays the resulting outcomes as an indication that the research reflected the most impact in increased focus and technical skills functional areas.

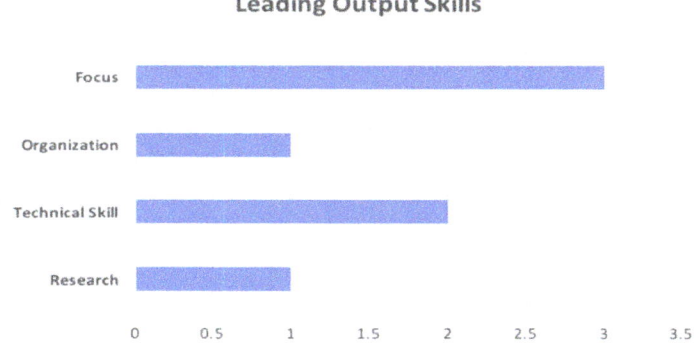

Figure 7-8 Leader Output Skills – Pilot Group

Success Leaders Influence

The business professionals and mentors encompassed a large portion of the results related to the Success Behaviors Research. Within organizations, senior leaders can offer a great deal of information and heavily influence followers based on their values and experiences as transferrable skills. Business professionals and mentors offer additional information that individuals can assess to determine an organization's benchmarks. The participants provided insight regarding the following areas: attributes related to personal success, factors contributing to success definitions, activities used to develop mental fortitude, behaviors for leader success, and recommendations for others aspiring to achieve success. The attributes function as supportive assets to the leader inputs as part of the *LeaderMind* theory methodology.

The business leaders identified support of family and cultural values, perseverance, and training as the leading concepts that contribute to individual success indicated in Figure 7-9.

Figure 7-9 Success Influencers – Leadership Group

In Figure 7-10, the business leaders also defined success related to developed skills and setting goals with a defined vision. The results represent the mindset of organizational leaders operating within the context of a positive cultural environment.

Figure 7-10 Success Definition – Leadership Group

The *LeaderMind* theory uses mental fortitude as an added component to leader success. Figure 7-11 captures the top activities that leaders utilize to support mental fortitude. Exercise, meditation and prayer, and the use of positive affirmations reflect the principal supportive constructs among successful business leaders represented in the Success Behaviors Research.

Mental Fortitude Builders-Leadership

Figure 7-11 Mental Fortitude Builders – Leadership Group

The business leaders also recommended advice to junior leaders seeking success. Setting goals and visions and perseverance were among the top traits reported when advising others desiring success achievement, as reflected in Figure 7-12. Identifying leading mental fortitude constructs would allow organizations to better formulate successful mental capacity strategies to support and equip constituents with the information needed to develop their foundational base.

Figure 7-12 Recommended Success Traits – Leadership Group

Research Limitations

The Success Behaviors Research gives an overview and tests the theories related to the *LeaderMind* model. Though the research addressed several aspects of success, experiences are cumulative and require additional research to observe the participants over a more extensive scope. The goals used were short-term to reflect a positive attitude toward achievement. Many factors, such as extended skill development requiring increased mental fortitude, cultural defects within organizations, and systemic behavioral issues related to lack of motivation and complex environmental stressors, would require additional research to formulate more defined data components.

Research Implications

The Success Behaviors Research simulates organizational development's environment with the structure of the

LeaderMind theory as a framework to address fostering success in leaders. The research protocols addressed many aspects of behavioral functions necessary in the development of success. The research began by addressing the behavioral factors related to success. Throughout the study and based on the resulting outputs, the research reflects new skill development, new behaviors, accountability, increased focus, and mental shifts as the leading components of research impact affecting the pilot group (See Figures 7-4, 7-5, and 7-8 below).

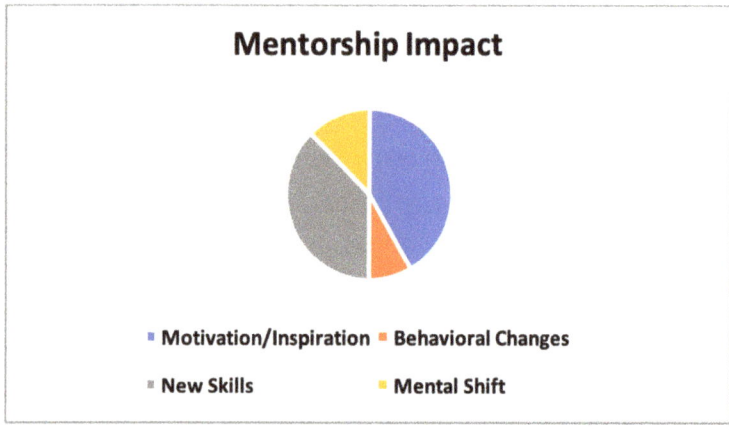

Figure 7-4 Mentorship Impact On Pilot Group

Leader/Training Influence Impact

- Motivational
- Behavioral Changes
- New Skills
- Increased Focus
- Accountability
- Mental Shift
- Unbiased Perspective

Figure 7-5 Leader/Training Impact On Pilot Group

The impact charts also reflect a high value placed on motivation in Figures 7-4 and 7-5. When thinking about work environments and the typical 40-hour workweek, people spend a large amount of their day surrounded by work peers. The impression leaders make on constituents affects more than just the bottom line. Leaders affect internal environments posed for collaborative innovation, extending into communities and eventually nations.[227] Success breeds success and creative impact starts with developing from within.

227   Charles Palus and David Horth. *The Leader's Edge: Six Creative Competencies for Navigating Complex Challemges*. (San Francisco: California: John Wiley & Sons, Inc., 2002), 8-9, 132-133.

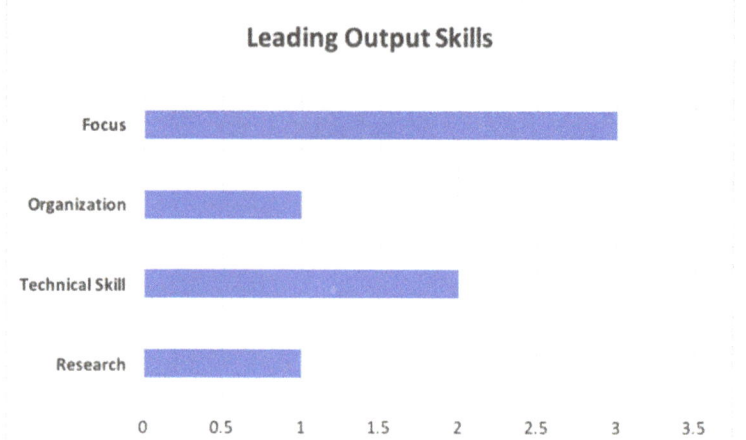

Figure 7-8 Leading Output Skills – Pilot Group

Success Behaviors Implications

The research implications related to the factors associated with the impact also determined the *LeaderMind* pillars related to **mentorship, leadership influence, and training** combined with **mental success behaviors** had the most significant effect on participant performance results. Individuals and organizations seeking to utilize this information would benefit from developing protocols related to such aspects of the *LeaderMind* theory when formulating plans for leadership development.

Perhaps you are wondering how you can start this growth process. Leadership or success development programs utilizing the *LeaderMind* pillars offer support for organizations wishing to create sustainable cultures based on encouraging leaders in their roles as supervisors and managers. When organizations move beyond basic levels of training to personalized growth and development through mentoring and self-assessed determinants, people begin to better understand their abilities and flourish. Encouraging internal awareness coupled with supportive action plans leads to positive behavioral changes at the individual and institutional levels. The common term, 'one-team, one-fight,' as a mindset becomes collaborative as organizations strive to see their people become more successful in personal and career arenas.

Mental Fortitude Implications

The *LeaderMind* theory addresses the behaviors related to developing a healthy mindset based on daily habits. The actions associated with the outcomes indicate a strong need for including mental fortitude as an additional component for supplementing the framework pillars. Achieving the practices associated with developing mental fortitude requires patience and time. Daily affirmations, meditation, and exercise are some of the possibilities organizations can use to supplement the leader development outcome. Activities centered around wellness and overall positive cultural environments would significantly affect the research period's results.

Mental fortitude is an aspect that senior managers should address throughout organizations. Leaving the issues related to mental stamina up to individuals places organizations in potentially detrimental situations. In their book *Do Business Better*, Damian Mason and Larry Winget suggest that 'When you allow emotion to run your business, emotion will ruin your business!'[228] Focusing on mental fortitude could have impacts that are far beyond individual constituents. Similar to behavioral development, a whole organization approach allows those in leadership an opportunity to encourage individual strengthening related to mental stamina, which can synergistically affect the organization's ability to sustain development and growth. Implementing a clear development plan to include parameters that address mental resilience, such as daily mental breaks, positive emails, or quarterly meetings focused on mental wellness, can be used to strengthen organizations from the inside out.

Additional Outcomes

During the research interviews conducted, the pilot group participants reported several unanticipated milestones. Two of the participants presented unanticipated achievements related to promotions and advanced academic achievement as a part of the research. For the others, the data appeared in the interview process in answers unrelated to the pilot group participants' questioned success outcomes. Additional research should address why some participants choose not to report their achievements under the auspices of the research questions related to achievement. Future research may link this information to issues associated with the 'bragging factor' addressed earlier. Research dictates that though many of the results appear as separate functions

---

228   Mason and Winget, 195.

from the anticipated research goals, the *LeaderMind* protocols influenced participants, as referenced in Table 7-1.

Unanticipated Participant Achievements	
Job Promotion	16%
Pursuing Additional Formal Education	32%
New Business Clientele	16%
Expanded Long-Term Goals Documented	16%

Table 7-1 Unanticipated Participant Achievements

Time Management and Perseverance

Throughout the Success Behaviors Research, the participants in the research group referred to issues involving time management. The perception in these cases is individuals can manage that time. Success strategies indicate that a better term would be to synchronize time and work to blend it into other functions. In the book *First Steps Toward Effective Time Management*, Patrick Forsyth supposes that by focusing on results and not merely achievement, time management functions can ensure success.[229] The business professionals and mentors participating in the study repeatedly referred to the perseverance and determination needed for success. Furthermore, Mason and Winget suggest that resolution moves people toward better choices in life.[230]

---

229   Patrick Forsyth. *First Steps Towards Effective Time Management.* (3rd ed.) (London: Kogan Page Ltd, 2013), 13-14.

230   Mason and Winget, 43.

Pushing yourself toward success can have tremendous effects on your achievements.

Preparation and Success

Other areas reflected through the Success Behaviors Research were indicative of preparation and its relationship to success. These factors are of critical importance when it comes to creating unique opportunities for success. The subject of preparation takes on its own role when it comes to getting ready to champion personal success. Later we will explore additional factors that individuals can use to prepare themselves to meet the challenges of achieving success with grace and stamina.

Business and Individual Implications

Within organizations, senior leaders may wish to develop their tract based on the research protocols represented. The *LeaderMind* theory encompasses several areas related to discovering purpose, mental fortitude, decision-making, and corrective action. When developing leaders, it is essential to assess each factor and include practices that offer support. Individuals can use the information separate from an organizational structure. However, consideration must foster a structured environment inclusive of the *LeaderMind* pillars related to **training, mentorship, leader influence, performance metrics, benchmark awareness, and organizational feedback** in pursuing success.

Mental Moments: Where Do We Go from Here?

The *LeaderMind* theory and Success Behaviors Research offer multiple information areas that individuals can use to assess personalized tracks related to developing success. The road to success is a patient and steady process. Introducing a success framework such as the *LeaderMind* theory coupled with mental fortitude allows better understanding when using success development plans. Mental fortitude combined with behavior can grow your success prospectus and lead to formidable results in multiple areas. You can use the following questions to address areas that will prepare you for the next phase on your journey toward success. Reflection upon your answers to the following questions will help you establish action steps to progress toward your dreams.

- How do you define success?
- Which skills are your strongest and weakest?
- What role can leader influence and training play in your success?
- Do you have an established routine comprised of positive daily habits?
- Are you committed to taking the next step and refining your action plan for success?

CHAPTER 8

SUCCESS AND INTENTIONS

The Power of Intent

An individual's intention is a powerful concept when it comes to focusing and mental stamina. It lives the hopes of thoughts, dreams, wonders, and the expectancy of what they will become. In the book *Living Zen Remindfully: Retraining Subconscious Awareness*, James Austin suggests that when an individual's focus desires to achieve a matter, the subconscious mind goes to work and delivers powerful results based on mental habits.[231] The hope is that those intentional ideas translate to actions centered around beneficial criteria to the thinker, for the subconscious mind knows no difference. In his research related to attitudes, intentions, and behaviors, Richard Bagozzi also supports intention as an act grounded in behavioral circumstances that move the initiator based on personal experience and a desire to change.[232] Without movement, the intention falls by the side only to be rooted in folly or happenstance and never see the light of day. So why do we need this focus anyway? Intention works hand in hand with desire and leaves much to be accomplished

---

231 James H. Austin. *Living Zen Remindfully: Retraining Subconscious Awareness*. (Cambridge, MA: The MIT Press, 2016), 78.

232 Richard P. Bagozzi. "The Self-Regulation of Attitudes, Intentions, and Behavior." *Social Psychology Quarterly* 55 no. 2 (1992): 184.

when missing.[233] Our motivation requires direction to execute actions. Furthermore, Bagozzi suggests that 'intentions and desire are not the same thing' and are 'distinct mental events.'[234] A person may have a desire to change. However, unless desire collaborates with the motivational factor of intent, the person may never achieve the status that they wish to attain.

Output Equals Input

Harvesting crops is in my blood. From an early age, I spent Saturday mornings on my grandparents' farm, helping in the garden well before the sun would rise. While my friends were busy eating cereal and watching Saturday morning cartoons, I was napping from the 5 a.m. start of my day. Those were some difficult years for me on the weekend as an adolescent. I had attended school all week and wanted nothing more than to sleep late. However, my grandparents instilled valuable life lessons in their grandchildren. They taught us the importance of consistency, dedication, hard work, and sacrifice. As children, my parents could buy my siblings and me nice clothing and Christmas gifts. I am convinced that this resulted from all the money they saved not having to shop in the local grocery store in the Fall when most people's gardens had grown astray. My grandmother would open her oversized freezer and happily distribute frozen vegetables and fresh meats to our immediate families and close relatives. As a grownup, I cherish those fond memories and

---

233   Ibid, 185.
234   Ibid, 185.

now understand that time was not just about the food we were harvesting. It was also about the iron-clad work ethics we learned. My understanding is that an individual's desired output is only as far as they are willing to reach.

> Do not be deceived: God cannot be mocked. A man reaps what he sows. Whoever sows to please their flesh, from the flesh will reap destruction; whoever sows to please the Spirit, from the Spirit will reap eternal life. Let us not become weary in doing good, for at the proper time we will reap a harvest if we do not give up. Therefore, as we have opportunity, let us do good to all people, especially to those who belong to the family of believers (Galatians 6:7-9, NIV).[235]

Galatians 6: 7-9 comes with a promise. The promise states that you get out what you put in, but only if you keep going. Perseverance void of perfectionism is the key to keep going. John Maxwell reminds us that God does not require perfection to work in our lives, only a willing heart to obey.[236] In *Running with the Giants*, John Maxwell further details a recap of Abraham's life and God's promise to bless him with many descendants, as reflected in the book of Genesis.[237] [238] According to Maxwell, Abraham was worried about whether God had chosen the right individual based on his mistakes.[239] For Abraham, there was also the concern regarding his

---

235   Gal. 6:7-9 (NIV).
236   Maxwell, 72.
237   Genesis 15:5 (God's Word Translation).
238   Maxwell, 65-74.
239   Ibid, 72.

> **YOU GET OUT WHAT YOU PUT IN, BUT ONLY IF YOU KEEP GOING.**

old age.[240] However, God was more concerned with Abraham's willingness to fulfill the calling in his life, based on trusting God's ability and not relying on his own.[241] [242] God blessed Abraham as promised, based on a reliable timeline that He established.[243] A person who maintains the course and encompasses the idea of winning will become a champion in the end, even if they are running at a slower pace.

The possibility of required change may release a sense of urgency in some and dread in others. Remaining focused on the output creates scenarios where comfort is associated with change. According to Peter Northouse in his book *Leadership: Theory and Practice*, people do not like to change and strive for equilibrium.[244] He further proposed that some may even engage in protagonistic behaviors such as avoiding tasks to maintain their lives' constant state.[245] Northouse also suggested remaining focused and disciplined regarding challenging concepts and work.[246] Change is not easy for some. However, we cannot avoid it or the circumstances that it brings. Change can bring new directions if we embrace those processes that allow momentum to grow in our lives.

---

240   Gen. 17:17 (GW).
241   Gen. 15:6 (GW).
242   Maxwell, 72-73.
243   Gen. 15:18; 21:2 (NIV).
244   Peter G. Northouse. *Leadership: Theory and practice.* Thousand Oaks, CA: SAGE Publications, 2016, 269.
245   Ibid, 269.
246   Ibid, 270.

Maintaining a fortified attitude and building a wall of perseverance also strengthens your performance.

Your Attitude is Going Places

As a child, I enjoyed reading Dr. Seuss's books. His books delivered just the right amount of semantics to make individuals think on their toes in rhythm. Today, I still own several *Dr.*  *Seuss* books. They keep me grounded and remind me not to take things so seriously when I glance at them sitting among the scholarly books in my office. When processes challenge my thinking, the simplicity offered in such writing provides clearer direction. When it came to attitude, Dr. Seuss suggested the following in deciding where to go in life:

> You have brains in your head. You have feet in your shoes. You can steer yourself any direction you choose. You're on your own. And you know what you know. And YOU are the guy who'll decide where to go.[247]

Many people have what I call the Monday morning syndrome. They dread the start of the week when it means that they have to do someone else's work. Let's face it, if you work regular work hours, you get approximately fifty-two mini-vacations each year, one at the end of each workweek. Many people spend that time doing a multitude of things. Some do chores, sleep, exercise, watch television, read a book, surf the internet, attend religious services, or eat. There is

---

247   Seuss, Dr. *Oh the Places You'll Go!* (New York: Random House, 1990).

a common thread here. They choose (in many cases) when it comes to their activities, how they spend their time. The beginning of the workweek means that they have to return to someone else's schedule, and the reality that their brief vacation has ended sets in on Sunday evening. According to Kouzes and Posner in their book *The Leadership Challenge: How to Make Extraordinary Things Happen in Organizations*, there is a solution to this thinking to help individuals view their jobs as springboards to propel them forward.[248] They summarize the idea of treating your career as an adventure and taking others along for the ride:

> Even if you've been in your job for years, treat today as if it were your first day. Ask yourself, 'If I were just starting this job, what would I do?' Begin doing those things now. Always stay alert to ways to improve your organization. Identify those projects that you have always wanted to undertake but never have. Ask your team members to do the same (p. 165).[249]

The authors wrote this advice with leaders in mind. However, the same mindset can be utilized by those seeking to make a difference in their lives and those of others. What can you change about your current situation? Perhaps you are self-employed or even domestically employed at home. These concepts are the same because the common thread lies in the attitude of the individual and how they choose to react in

---

248   Kouzes and Posner, 165.
249   Ibid.

the face of discipline and dedication.[250] An individual either chooses to invest or shrinks back in despair. The winner's circle would see everyone take the stance of stark fighter and defender of what is possible.

Small Steps Lead to Big Rewards

Like most people, I started my academic studies in kindergarten. I specifically remember my time spent on the playground. I also remember the birth of my creative mindset and the support that I received from my teachers. I drew the cover for the school's Christmas play program that year. I still remember how excited I was when my teacher delivered the fantastic news to my mother during the parent-teacher conference. My mother was excited as well. It was the beginning of a process that has led me to an innovative mindset in everything that I do. At the time, I could never have dreamed of pursuing a doctorate. That vision was birthed in my mind over time. Individuals paved the support network that created the environment for me to grow because they were willing to deposit what I like to think of as wisdom nuggets. Those inputs have been the culmination of many years of investment in a young woman's future. The adage 'eating the elephant one bite at a time' still works.

A piecemeal process may not be the desire of those taking the fast route. After all, no one wants to win the lottery by receiving a one hundred-million-dollar jackpot one day at a time. It would take one hundred million days,

---

250   Kouzes and Posner, 165.

or approximately 273,973 years, to collect your reward before taxes. Speeding up the return rate is desirable if you remember that there are invaluable lessons to be learned along the way. Skipping over the less desirable parts of the journey can foster a foundation that lacks needed resources for the future. The *LeaderMind* theory supposes a framework that maintains progress with minimal distraction. However, the process requires personal responsibility to achieve the journey.

Using the example of the value of small steps in a successful business destined for growth, Hank Moore (2019) proposes the following in his book *The Big Picture of Business: Big Ideas and Strategies: 7 Steps Toward Business Success*:

> The public company that sustains high book value must demonstrate its ability to focus on depth-and-substance, not just on flash-and-sizzle. Those that proclaim that hot ideas make great stock tips are dreamers selling flavors of the month, not companies with staying power. Taking a company public must be a process of guiding the organization through the levels of accomplishment. Sustaining book value is a thorough progression. Management must develop critical thinking skills, through organizational processes, problem solving, challenges to take risks and daring to innovate.[251]

Part of the process for success entails using the framework that guides actions. In her research related to organizational

---

251   Hank Moore. *The Big Picture of Business: Big Ideas and Strategies: 7 Steps Toward Business Success.* (Newburyport: Morgan James Publishing, 2019).

success, Sherri McMillan suggests that structured plans ensure that movement directs the goal and achievement of process steps along the way.[252] Multiple avenues of success exist. However, framing your objectives around an end goal allows you to focus on the prize.

Realizing the Big Picture

Directing your thoughts toward an overall focus is paramount to success. Allison Maslan details the external viewpoint in her book *Scale or Fail: How to Build Your Dream Team, Explode Your Growth and Let Your Business Soar*, noting that when others look at your goals, they should be able to describe your passions and the steps it will take to get there.[253] Although I am no expert at figure skating, I suppose that it takes a lot of time spent on the ice practicing to reach the Olympics. I remember having dreams of being an ice skater at the Olympics. As a result, I signed my daughter up for classes when she was young. She entertained the idea for a while. However, her passion is in animation, and her support of my dream to ice skate was over after one practice season. My daughter's purpose of making others happy framed her love of drawing with several years of training. When she was eight years old, I had her write out action steps to help her reach her goals. I asked her what she would like to do in life. She gleamed with excitement about becoming a cartoonist. As her

---

252   Sherri McMillan. "Focus on the Big Picture for Fitness Business Success." *Club Industry* (2013).

253   Allison Maslan. *Scale Or Fail: How to Build Your Dream Team, Explode Your Growth, and Let Your Business Soar*. (Newark: John Wiley & Sons, Incorporated, 2018), 37.

parent, I want her to be successful. I asked her to tell me how she thought she would arrive at that goal. Through a series of steps, we detailed a written plan working from the big picture (or result) backward: get a job as a cartoonist, graduate from college, graduate from high school, graduate from elementary and middle school, pass the third grade, and complete homework. The next week, I took her to a local college and explained that one day, she would attend a university of her choice to share a tangible vision that she could focus on.

We started the vision process when she was young. The plan was simple but detailed a series of steps that she has followed as she continues to pursue her goals as a college student. Can reaching goals be as simple as looking toward desired results? In the book *The Big Picture of Business, Big Ideas and Strategies: 7 Steps Toward Business Success*, Hank Moore has concluded that most businesses do not focus on the big picture and instead often waste time avoiding the actions that can drive success while focusing on emergency contingencies that misalign focus (2019).[254] Emergencies are important. However, moving beyond such attitudes is equally essential. Mentioning the idea of a big picture means that we must have a goal-setting objective or an area of focus.

Goal-Setting and Passion

Earlier we focused on discovering purpose and our God-given pursuits centered around a life dedicated to God, in service

---

254   Hank Moore. *The Big Picture of Business, Big Ideas and Strategies: 7 Steps Toward Business Success.* (Newburyport: Morgan James Publishing, 2019).

to others. But how do we set our goals? How do we determine what we should do in service to others? Sometimes we need assistance with areas where we may not have full awareness. Of course, mentors and coaches can assist with that discovery process, and we will continue to explore this concept moving forward.

People have often mentioned that they don't know how to set goals that they can finish. Have you ever started a project only to find yourself sidetracked? Perhaps you even made it halfway through the plan and did not know how to finish. Using your Master Key requires a plan worth achieving. Maslan supports that visualization can release actions in our mind that induce activity.[255]

Additionally, being attuned to the process of living in the present moment can help achieve a connection to our minds by releasing feelings that cause us to misjudge situations and limit our responses.[256] Furthermore, Maslan (2018) uses a multilevel approach to visualize the business you desire.[257] Maslan proposes the 'Big Picture Mind Map' to understand the details of an optimal future that combines recording expectancies through a series of questions directed toward envisioning the process for a successful business through relaxed and creative mind flow (p. 43).[258] Below is a brief exercise inspired by the 'Big Picture Mind Map' with some

255 Maslan, 46.
256 Liz Hall. *Mindful Coaching: How Mindfulness Can Transform Coaching Practice.* (London: Kogan Page, 2013), 14.
257 Maslan, 42-45.
258 Ibid, 43.

added details to assist you with the process of determining an area of focus to direct your goals (p. 43).[259]

> Find a quiet space where you can sit and relax. Take a moment to think about your future. While envisioning your future, think about your best-looking attire and the home of your dreams. What do you want it to look like? How does it feel? What kind of clothes are you wearing? Now, think of your dream job. The one job that you would love to do all day. What would you be doing, especially if you knew you could set your salary? No matter which career you choose, the pay is more than $150K per year. So be limitless in your choice. Where do you work, and how often? See yourself driving to your place of business and smiling with joy as you walk into the building.

You have just tapped into something powerful: your passion. Discovering your passion will create a goal that moves you beyond the ordinary. The plan you use to get there is simply a conduit to take you from the passion to the reality you envisioned.[260] Next, detail the steps that you think it will take for you to reach your vision. It does not matter if the steps are accurate at this point. What matters is getting them on paper. By writing your goals down, you open yourself up to opportunities. In his book *Planning a Successful Future: Managing to Be Wealthy for Individuals and Their Advisors*, John Sestina suggests that written goals are another part of designing a framework for success because they create

---

259 Ibid.
260 Ibid, 41.

a chance to devise a plan that will stick.[261] Written goals create an opportunity to identify gaps, tell others what you want so that they can support you, and give you a frame of reference to review to ensure that you remain focused.[262] Moving forward, we will learn the process of defining your action steps to success. In the book of Habakkuk, the Bible encourages us to write out our vision and keep the process simple while we are working through goals:

> Then the Lord answered me,
> 'Write the vision.
> Make it clear on tablets
> so that anyone can read it quickly.
> The vision will still happen at the appointed time.
> It hurries toward its goal.
> It won't be a lie.
> If it's delayed, wait for it.
> It will certainly happen.
> It won't be late.'[263]

The Support Foundation For Growth

Without the right direction, a bridge can end up going nowhere fast, especially when the going gets tough. Creating a framework for assistance means opening the mind up to expanded opportunities for growth. The *LeaderMind*

---

261   John E. Sestina. *Planning a Successful Future: Managing to Be Wealthy for Individuals and Their Advisors*. (Hoboken: John Wiley & Sons, Inc., 2016), 19.

262   Sestina, 19-20.

263   Hab. 2:2-3 (GW).

theory supposes that the supportive structure facilitates a proven track to assist with directed achievement. As you move forward, begin to think of individuals who can support you on your road to success.

Mental Moments: Where Do We Go from Here?

Determining a clear path to success starts with directing your thoughts. It would help if you also decided which direction you will go and how to get there. Detailing the action steps can be simple if you know what you are accomplishing. Give yourself the freedom to dream and determine your realities in life. The decisions of others do not bind you. You are as free as you allow yourself to be. Using the Master Key theory addresses the momentum to change directions if needed based on your visions. The journey to success includes many processes. Determine the big picture by connecting with your passion, much like connecting the dots in a picture puzzle along 'your' logical path. This process can help you create a support network to achieve your goals. For now, the following questions will help you identify steps that will connect your intentions to dreams and your dreams into actions:

- Which intentions are you using to guide your actions?
- What kind of efforts are you using to achieve processes?
- What does your big picture of success entail?
- Have you connected with your passion?
- Have you identified the smaller steps on your way to success?
- Have you created a written plan for your goals?

CHAPTER 9

COACHES AND MENTORS

The *LeaderMind* theory encompasses the use of mentors in the process of leadership development. As we have progressed, the idea of guidance as a critical step in your success process has been intentionally mentioned as a matter of positive reinforcement. Partnering with others can provide different perspectives and greater insight. When we do things on our own, have we determined that we know the process well enough to get from one point to another? However, is the matter of considering yourself an expert relative to the task? I will admit that I did not know everything about raising my child. Unfortunately, they do not come with operation manuals. Whether it is childrearing or another task such as cooking, some people like to think of themselves as experts.

In some cases, people are very proficient, and in others, they are not. Sestina suggests that we are not experts at everything in life.[264] We must understand that when we get assistance to reach a goal, we increase our chances of success, often with less invasive obstacles than those encountered by the people who lived before us. Wise decisions prevail when

---

264   Sestina, 164.

we hire people who are subject matter experts.[265] History has proven to be a provider of wisdom.

Why Mentors Matter

There are dedicated people in the world who can impart wisdom and help facilitate ideas. Peddy encourages us that mentors help others achieve their goals by identifying constructs such as insight, decision-making, hardiness, and individuality.[266] Mentors can also more readily assess a situation to determine the best course of action.[267] Additionally, mentors may get into the intimate details of your life at times to help you get to where you are going. They are effective at setting examples that others can follow.[268] Making the most of what a mentor offers can put you on the road to success. However, who are these individuals, and where can you find them?

Mentors can come from everywhere. According to Andrew Miller in his book *Mentoring Students and Young People: A Handbook of Effective Practice*, mentors exist in communities in the form of peers who usually work to distribute similar skill levels.[269] However, they possess strategic qualities that position them to assist others effectively. Mentors help

---

265   Ibid, 164.
266   Peddy, 2.
267   Ibid, 3.
268   Ibid, 3.
269   Andrew Miller. *Mentoring Students and Young People: A Handbook of Effective Practice*. (Abingdon, Oxon: Taylor & Francis Group, 2002), 87, 126.

people by showing them how to operate in their environment.[270] They understand the rules of a given operation and know how to point out missing areas that others need to follow based on logic.[271] Mentoring

PREPARING OTHERS FOR THE ROAD AHEAD BECOMES ESPECIALLY IMPORTANT WHEN IT COMES TO FUTURE LEADERS.

also affects self-growth. In their research related to adolescence learning, Mike Younger and Molly Warrington suppose the idea that mentorship coupled with strategic goals affects self-confidence and educational ambitions.[272] Peddy also adds that mentors should use leadership as an example to pass on values and lessons that can assist others in the challenges that they may face.[273]

Preparing others for the road ahead becomes especially important when it comes to future leaders. In his book *Effective Succession Planning: Ensuring Leadership Continuity and Building Succession Planning from Within*, William Rothwell notes that as organizations face crises in how to govern themselves in the future, planning can mean the difference in creating a viable path to organizational sustainability through knowledge retention and critical players.[274] Preparing leaders is contingent on creating scenarios where ethics are prime as

---

270   Ibid, 2.

271   Ibid, 2.

272   Mike Younger and Molly Warrington. "Mentoring and Target-Setting in a Secondary School in England: An Evaluation of Aims and Benefits." *Oxford Review of Education* 35, no. 2 (2009): 177.

273   Peddy, 126.

274   William J. Rothwell. *Effective Succession Planning: Ensuring Leadership Continuity and Building Talent from Within*. (New York, New York: Amacom, 2016), xxi.

expressed in values, proficiency, and performance, whether operating internally or externally in their work environment.[275] Peddy also references the thought that mentors help others see their behaviors, review options, share experiences, and offer instruction when it is requested.[276] Aditya Simha and Praveen Parboteeah's research of unethical practices and identifying personality-associated types address the idea that a misbalance between performance expectations and ethics can sway individuals to utilize unethical practices.[277] Such criteria suggest that ethical examples are important in societies that value performance metrics over everything else. Mentors can act as the light that keeps individuals on track with processes and value determinations.

There are situations where mentorship can develop from family members. My grandparents were successful at impacting my entire generation by helping us see the value in working hard to achieve lifelong goals. Peddy notes that such role models are essential as we begin the process of achievement.[278] Kouzes and Posner also support that providing a positive example also shows you that a mentor is committed to their ideals and can serve as an expert in their area of expertise.[279] Leaders promote credibility when they demonstrate espoused values that reflect what they

---

275   Ibid, 102.

276   Peddy, 60-61.

277   Aditya Simha and Praveen Parboteeah K. "The Big 5 Personality Traits and Willingness to Justify Unethical Behavior—A Cross-National Examination: JBE." *Journal of Business Ethics*: 1-21 (2019): 7.

278   Peddy, 152.

279   Kouzes and Posner, 74.

desire to teach others.[280] Look for examples found in the success areas that you are working on.

Unfortunately, family members or friends can also act out of selfishness and not serve as good mentors. John Sestina warns of such actions as they concern the athletes he advises in his book *Planning a Successful Future: Managing to Be Wealthy for Individuals and Their Advisors*.[281] His recommendation includes avoiding the guidance of family members who only have selfish ambitions or lack the knowledge to substantiate successful financial practices based on their lack of awareness regarding wealth.[282] Sestina further advises that selecting role models based on familiar loyalty can lead to faulty investments or loss of wealth.[283] Choosing the right partners within your quest for achievement is a critical step. According to Shulz and Yang, Howard Shultz almost lost the opportunity to purchase Starbucks.[284] Shultz entered the meeting of a lifetime with Bill Gates Sr., of all individuals, as a partner in his quest.[285] However, even having the experience of a knowledgeable businessperson could not prepare him for the ridicule Shultz would experience on his road to success. Because of his values and supportive investment partners, Shultz raised the capital needed and secured a deal to purchase Starbucks.[286] He accomplished the task

---

280　Ibid, 74.
281　Sestina, 162.
282　Ibid, 162.
283　Ibid.
284　Shultz and Yang, 92.
285　Ibid, 92-93.
286　Ibid.

with dignity and his values intact and positively affected the investments of those around him in the process.[287] Whether it comes to money or other professional development areas, competency and values matter when choosing advisors.

Coaches as Cheerleaders

I remember being a cheerleader in elementary school. It was one of the most fantastic times of my life. I loved to perform, but I was quiet. Cheerleading allowed me to be someone else. I could encourage others, the football players and the fans, as the game progressed on the field. Those years included cold nights full of hot cocoa and little huddles of smartly dressed girls trying to stay warm. Years later, I would get that same rush of excitement as part of my high school's marching band. Providing support for the team was a big part of my adolescent years. I wanted to see my school win in every sport that I supported. Seeing people win sparked something deep inside of me. It is still there today. When I observe someone reaching a goal that I know they have worked their whole life to achieve, I often get goosebumps. I cherish the opportunity to partner with others in reaching their goals. Whether it is a brief conversation or a shared relationship, achievement in others and equality are two of my most prominent enjoyment areas.

Everyone wants to win, and organizations want to hire these winners. However, what happens when you hire the best player and place them in the game without a coach?

---

287   Ibid, 93.

How effective can a team be without coaches to guide the path? The games of life and business are complex, with shifting plays around every corner, much like sports. Because the goal of most games is to hold the trophy at the end, coaching becomes critical. According to Robert Hargrove, he shares in his book *Masterful Coaching,* that effective coaching entails developing a winning strategy that progresses individuals to move along the path with skill and strategy while increasing the score to the champion's circle.[288] Coaches also act as change agents.[289] Sometimes, the changes come in the form of new rules or outcomes. Coaches can also help you determine which paths to take. However, it is still up to you to execute the strategies.

Coaches possess innate qualities that make them great in the game of life. According to Collins, they lead others somewhere based on the skills and talents that they own.[290] They also understand their core values, are excellent at relating to people, work on timetables that produce outcomes, are creative, and maintain their commitments with alignment to their viewpoints.[291] Sometimes, people get themselves into situations that require a sharp vision to move forward and achieve. Coaches who offer the strategies to get them there bring encouragement and constructive criticism as relational factors that allow people to maintain

---

288   Robert Hargrove. *Masterful Coaching.* (3rd ed.) (San Francisco: California; Jossey-Bass, 2008), 14-15.
289   Ibid, 15.
290   Collins, 40.
291   Ibid, 34-38.

their individuality.[292] Hargrove supposes that coaches also master the art of conversations that invite people to share experiences, develop strategies, and are encouraged to act.[293] The best motivational speeches that I have witnessed were in the locker room during high school when the team was down several points on the scoreboard. Coaches can change the direction of the game by cheering differently and shifting strategies when needed.

Have you ever seen community teams play sports? While watching my daughter's junior basketball league play, I learned an essential aspect of good coaching. The coach allowed every child an equal amount of playtime in the game. The coach was committed to ensuring that every child walked away from that game feeling like a winner. Each child was developing at different skill levels. However, they all had an opportunity to improve. The coach's strategy during the process of the game was to focus more on the individual progress of each team player versus the scoreboard at the end of each game. Of course, teams want to win. Coaches ensure that everyone does their part to make sure the team wins, according to Collins.[294] Coaching is a give-and-take situation. Coaches who dedicate themselves to the process end up with committed players in return. In their research related to productivity and coaching, Joseph Mosca, Alan Fazzari, and John Buzza support that developing others requires an in-depth analysis of strengths and

---

292   Ibid, 41.
293   Hargrove, 92
294   Collins, 43.

potential assessed over time.[295] Eventually, the scoreboard catches up to an individual's improved skill set, resulting in a win-win situation. According to Hall, coaches also help people personally by allowing them to better understand the inner thought processes that help them adjust paradigms based on past experiences.[296] Ultimately, coaches transfer their expertise to others through strategies that develop performance and shared commitments to succeed.

Coach or Mentor?

According to Magnus Klofsten and Staffan Öberg's research differentiating coaching and mentoring, they are different, though they can work on a tangent.[297] Both processes provide guidance and helpful feedback when leading others toward a critical outcome.[298] Coaching strategies are generally more formal and depend on agreeable meeting structures that document the process.[299] Mentoring relationships focus more on suggesting outcomes that others can follow.[300] Mentoring relationships also focus on solving specific issues, while coaching establishes protocols that affect processes.[301]

---

295 Joseph B. Mosca, Alan Fazzari, and John Buzza. "Coaching to Win: A Systematic Approach to Achieving Productivity through Coaching." *Journal of Business & Economics Research* 8, no. 5 (2010): 122.

296 Hall, 13.

297 Magnus Klofsten and Staffan Öberg. "Coaching Versus Mentoring: Are there any Differences?" Emerald Group Publishing Limited. 9 (2012): 39.

298 Ibid, 42.

299 Ibid, 43.

300 Ibid.

301 Ibid.

Mentoring involves coaching and vice versa, meaning that they intersect at various points.[302] Selecting a mentor or coach should involve choosing someone that aligns with your core values' important parts. Guidance assists individuals with processes that they may not fully comprehend. Mentors have a background in specific industry processes as subject matter experts, while coaches tend to focus on general backgrounds founded on business principles.[303] Ultimately, both relationships require engagement from the participants to encourage successful outcomes.[304] Choosing one over the other is dependent upon the situation and the goal of the individual.

The African proverb, 'It takes a village to raise a child,' places focus on the communal aspect of coaching and mentoring. Collins suggests that coaching requires a relational commitment that reveals several aspects of one's life.[305] It reveals areas of misguidance or distraction that need training or, in some instances, retraining.[306] According to Peddy, when mentoring others, feedback should offer edification.[307] Collins also suggests that while the coaching process provides results, its real value is reflected in the lives transformed.[308] Both approaches can be beneficial to success. Miller also suggests that mentorship offers the benefit of continued connection, positioning others in roles where

---

302   Ibid, 39.
303   Ibid, 45.
304   Klofsten and Öberg, 45.
305   Collins, 93.
306   Ibid, 96.
307   Peddy, 59.
308   Collins, 286.

they work in strategic capacities to mentor others, especially related to multi-generational learning, and the advantages of promoting the continued relationship between older and younger generations.[309] Coaches and mentors play a role in helping people change by developing individual strengths that can successfully transform societies.

Mental Moments: Where Do We Go from Here?

We do not exist in society by ourselves. The experiences of others can help us in creating paths to success. Coaches and mentors exist to create situations that propel us toward our desires. It takes commitment on our part when it comes to establishing relationships that can assist the process. Ultimately, no one can do the work for us. Choosing a mentor or coach requires selective methods based on the type of situation we desire to achieve and the development framework we decide to utilize. Ultimately, the goal is to produce momentum. The following questions will help develop the directional need when choosing a mentor or coach to help you achieve your goal.

- Have you determined the gaps in your plan that may require assistance?
- What details define a great coach or mentor to you?
- Are you focused on solving a process or a scenario?
- Have you determined the value that a coach or mentor can add?

---

309   Miller 274.

CHAPTER 10

MENTAL SUCCESS AND ACTION

Have you ever taken a driver's test? I remember taking the test for the first time as a teenager. I was nervous because I was a late bloomer in my circle of friends. Many of my friends had acquired their driver's licenses while they were in high school. However, I was a little younger than most of my friends and graduated when I was 17. During sophomore year, I had not reached the legal age to drive and did not see a need to rush. After high school, my social interests changed drastically, and having my license offered me the freedom to hang out and socialize on my timetable.

Preparing for the test, in my mind, was simple. I needed to study and practice a few times, and I was sure I would pass. Taking the written test was easy. Test-taking was an area where my studious traits shined. However, the practical test required application and I had not developed the skills needed to drive with proficiency. So, the first time I took the test, I failed. My mom assured me that I would do better the next time. Before I returned, I ensured that I had perfected the skills needed: three-point turn, using signals, and hands placed appropriately on the steering wheel. The second time that I took the test, I passed with ease. What changed? I did. I determined that I would pass the test the second time and did everything I needed to prepare.

In several stories, I have referenced some form of driving on the open road, whether mindlessly or taking bridges that lead us to destiny. The concept of driving is simple. If you want to get somewhere, it is a pretty good mode of transportation. However, the road trip will only be as great as the driver behind the car's wheel. If you want to perform at an optimal level, you must prepare for the bumps and knots that may lie ahead.

At the end of each chapter, the mental moments offered the chance to create a palette of choices that you can now use to set your own goals and draw your map. On the road to success, there are many pit stops. These areas offer reprieve and a place for you to restore. Before you head out on your journey, let's start with the right supplies.

♨ Mental Fortitude:

Developing your mental fortitude is dependent upon your daily habits. Have you established a plan to include positive interjections into your day? Erasing old mindsets that are limiting your performance may take some time. However, starting the process will initiate actions that can change your perspective of the world and your life. Do not limit yourself to the areas that you use consistently. Because you are reading this book, we can assume that reading may be an activity you enjoy. However, there are several ways to interject positive daily actions that affect your thinking into your day. You can start by incorporating music, podcasts, and audiobooks. You can use written notecards to display your affirmations by placing them in locations you frequent throughout the day. The steps may seem simple, yet the rewards are profound.

♨ Defined Purpose and Passion:

The steps to reach your passion are within your thoughts and imagination. Realizing that God created you with a purpose is the first step to obtaining success. Once you understand that God's love for you is so strong that He would not dare let you fail, your direction becomes clear. He promises in the book of Jeremiah that He has significant plans for your future: 'For I know the plans I have for you,' declares the Lord,' plans to prosper you and not to harm you, plans to give you hope and a future.'[310] God wants you to connect to your dreams, passions, and goals. God wants to inspire you

---

310   Jer. 29:11 (NIV).

to bring Him glory as you serve others, His people. If you have not connected to your passion, I encourage you to re-visit the exercise in Chapter 8 and allow yourself to dream. Starting with your vision, you can focus on the remainder of the steps needed to become successful.

🚗 Training:

Now that you have identified your true passion, it is time to develop your skills. God has already equipped you with what you need to achieve success. You only need to identify those skills and build upon them. For some, this can be quite a challenge. In his book *Strength Finder 2.0*, Tom Rath offers some healthy advice to summarize the quest of identifying your talent:

'You cannot be anything you want to be - but you can be a lot more of who you already are' (p.9).[311]

Rath successfully demonstrates the critical analysis of identifying your core strengths using themes.[312] Using tools such as the Strength Finder 2.0 Assessment can help you clearly distinguish your skills and determine the areas that can best support your passion.[313] You can start by writing down the skills that you feel are your strongest and add additional supportive information as you identify new ways to discover your gifts and talents.

---

311   Tom Rath. *Strengths Finder 2.0.* (New York, New York: Gallup Press, 2007), 9.
312   Rath, 16.
313   Ibid, 32.

🚗 Supportive Network:

Training is one of the components that will lead you to success. The other portion is the guidance that you receive. We cannot always choose our family. However, we do have a choice regarding the people that we allow to speak into our minds. Understanding the importance of leadership as the core of influence will grant you the posture to choose wisely.

Additionally, you will need to determine if you require help with processing or only need help in a specific area. Coaches and mentors are great for assisting you with the necessary guidance to move forward. Perhaps you work in an environment where mentors are assigned, such as the military. You are already one step ahead. If your passions reflect choices outside of your chosen career field, consider looking for mentors in the areas related to your goals. Chapter 9 offers additional insight to consider when selecting a coach or a mentor to assist you with your achievements. You may also want to consider several resources in your local community, such as churches or civic groups that aid those seeking guidance in multiple areas. For specialized services, do not be afraid to empower yourself. You are valuable and worth the investment.

🚗 Perseverance:

Winning the game in life and becoming a mental mogul is about more than showing up. It requires a mind that is determined to win, no matter what. The star player on the field is you. You have the chance to win for yourself when you 'show up and show out.' What does this term mean to you? The way that you approach success will determine both your level of altitude and aptitude. We have addressed all the tools reflected in your behaviors to get you to your destination. The tools to get to your destination: the car, the training, and the guidance will help you succeed. These ideals reflect your **purpose, passion, skills, leadership, and fortified mental stamina**. Your behaviors are the fuel for your car, and you can choose how much fuel or power you will need to get to your destination based on your determination. How determined are you to reach your goal? Connecting to your passion will allow you to focus on the road ahead and desire to get to your destination. Your map encompasses all the pit stops along the way. However, you hold the key to the power of your mind. Now, it is up to you to *use your Master Key* and *turn on the engine* that starts the process: *driving toward your destiny of success.*

BIBLIOGRAPHY

Airun, Anand. "Prepare Plants to Soak in Nourishment during Rains: Happy GARDENING." *DNA (Mumbai, India)*. (2016).

Ash, Mary K. *Mary Kay Ash: Miracles Happen*. (3rd ed.). NewYork: New York: Harper Perennial, 1994.

Austin, James H. *Living Zen Remindfully: Retraining Subconscious Awareness*. Cambridge, Massachusetts: The MIT Press, 2016.

Babbie, Earl. *The Practice of Social Research*. Belmont: California, 2004.

Badaracco, Joseph L. *Defining Moments: When Managers Must Choose Between Right and Right*. Boston, Massachusetts: Harvard Business School Press, 1997.

Bagozzi. Richard P. "The Self-Regulation of Attitudes, Intentions, and Behavior." *Social Psychology Quarterly* 55 no. 2 (1992): 178-204.

Bianco, Arnie. *One-Minute Discipline: Classroom Management Strategies that Work*. San Francisco, CA: Jossey-Bass, 2002.

Byers, Charity and John Walker. *Unhindered: Aligning the Story of Your Heart*. Carol Stream: AVAIL, 2020.

Caligiuri, Paula. *Cultural Agility: Building a Pipeline of Successful Global Professionals*. San Franciso: California: Jossey-Bass, 2012.

Chand, Samuel. *The Secret to Success: Three O's That Will Take You Anywhere in Life*. New Kensington, Pennsylvania: Whitaker House, 2020.

Chand, Samuel, and Cecil Murphy. *Who's Holding Your Ladder: Leadership's Most Critical Decision - Selecting Your Leaders*. Niles, Illinois: Mall Publishing Company, 2003.

Clinton, J. Robert. *The Making of a Leader: Recognizing the Lessons and Stages of Leadership Development*. Colorado Springs: Colorado: NavPress, 1988.

Coffey, Margaret, Nancy Lamport, and Gayle Hersch. *Creative Engagement in Occupation: Building Professional Skills*. Slack Incorporated, 2015.

Coley, Loretta. "Developing the Global Leader Mindset". LDSL 733. *Regent University*, Unpublished Essay, 2020.

Collins, Gary R. *Christian Coaching: Helping Others Turn Potential into Reality*. Colorado Springs: Colorado: NavPress, 2002.

Collins, Jim, and Jerry I. Porras. *Built to Last: Successful Habits of Visionary Companies*. New York: Harper Collins, 1997.

Converse, Patrick D., and Katrina A. Piccone, & Michael C. Tocci, "Childhood Self-control, Adolescent Behavior, and Career Success", *Personality and individual differences,* 59 (2014): 65-70.

Cook, Gareth. "Self-Control in Childhood Brings Future Success: Self-Control in Childhood Predicts Future Success." *The Boston Globe.* (2011), 1.

Covey, Steven R. The 7 *Habits of Highly Effective People: Restoring The Character Ethic.* New York: Free Press, 1989.

Cremades, Alejandro. *The Art of Startup Fundraising: Pitching Investors, Negotiating the Deal, and Everything Else Entrepreneurs Need to Know.* Hoboken, New Jersey: John Wiley & Sons, Inc., 2016.

Crocker, Jennifer, Yu Niiya, and Dominik Mischkowski. 2008. "Why does Writing about Important Values Reduce Defensiveness? Self-Affirmation and the Role of Positive Other-Directed Feelings." *Psychological Science* 19, no. 7 (2008): 740-747.

Daft, Richard. *Organization Theory & Design* (12 ed.). Boston: Massachusetts, 2016.

De Marneffe, Daphne. *Maternal Desire: On Children, Love, and the Inner Life.* New York, New York: Time Warner Books, 2004.

Epton, Tracy, Peter R. Harris, Rachel Kane, Guido M. van Koningsbruggen, and Paschal Sheeran. "The Impact of Self-Affirmation on Health-Behavior Change: A Meta-Analysis." *Health Psychology* 34, no. 3 (2015): 187-196.

Etzioni, Amitai. "The Moral Wrestler: Ignored by Maslow." *Society* 54, no. 6 (2017): 512-519.

Forsyth, Patrick. *First Steps Towards Effective Time Management.* (3rd ed.) London: Kogan Page Ltd, 2013.

Godfrey, Christina M., Margaret B. Harrison, Rosemary Lysaght, Marianne Lamb, Ian D. Graham, and Patricia Oakley. 2011. "Care of Self – Care by Other – Care of Other: The Meaning of Self-Care from Research, Practice, Policy and Industry Perspectives." *International Journal of Evidence-Based Healthcare* 9, no. 1 (2011): 3-24.

Hall, Liz. *Mindful Coaching: How Mindfulness Can Transform Coaching Practice.* London: Kogan Page, 2013.

Hanzén, Maria. "When in Rome, Do as The Romans Do: Proverbs as a Part of EFL Teaching" diss., Jönköping University, 2007. *DiVA.*

Hargrove, Robert. *Masterful Coaching.* (3rd ed.) San Francisco: California; Jossey-Bass, 2008.

Iger, Robert. *The Ride of a Lifetime: Lessons Learned From 15 Years as CEO of the Walt Disney Company.* New York: Random House, 2019.

Isaacson, Walter. "The Real Leadership Lessons of Steve Jobs." *Harvard Business Review* 90, no. 4 (2019): 92-102.

Klofsten, Magnus and Staffan Öberg. "Coaching Versus Mentoring: Are there any Differences?" *Emerald Group Publishing Limited.* 9 (2012): 39-47.

Kouzes, James and Barry Posner. *The Leadership Challenge: How to Make Extraordinary Things Happen in Organizations* (5th ed.). San Francisco, California: The Leadership Challenge, 2012.

Ladd, Carol, Grace Ladd, and Joy Ladd. *The Power of a Positive Teen.* New York: Howard Books, 2005.

Lee. Li-Yueh and Chia-Ying Li. "The Moderating Effects of Teaching Method, Learning Style and Cross-Cultural Differences on the Relationship between Expatriate Training and Training Effectiveness." *International Journal of Human Resource Management* 19, no. 4 (2008): 600-619.

Ley, Emily. *Grace Not Perfection: Embracing Simplicity, Celebrating Joy.* Nashville: Thomas Nelson, 2016.

Limb, Peter. *Nelson Mandela: A Biography.* Westport, Conn.: Greenwood, 2008.

Lyod, Alexander. *The Love Code: The Secret Principle to Achieving Success in Life, Love, and Happiness.* New York: Harmony Books, 2015.

Mallén, Fermin, Ricardo Chiva, Joaquin Alegre, and Jacob Guinot. "Are Altruistic Leaders Worthy? the Role of Organizational Learning Capability." *International Journal of Manpower* 36, no.3 (2015): 273.

Maslan, Allison. *Scale or Fail: How to Build Your Dream Team, Explode Your Growth, and Let Your Business Soar.* Newark: John Wiley & Sons, Incorporated, 2018.

Mason, Damian, and Larry Winget. *Do Business Better: Traits, Habits, and Actions to Help You Succeed.* Newark, New Jersey: John Wiley & Sons, Inc., 2019.

Maxwell, John C. *Running with the Giants: What Old Testament Heroes Want You to Know About Life and Leadership.* California: Warner Books, 2002.

McAllum, Kirstie. "Managing Imposter Syndrome among the "Trophy Kids": Creating Teaching Practices that Develop Independence in Millennial Students." *Communication Education* 65, no. 3 (2016): 363-365.

Mclachlan, Zak. "What is Success." *Wainwright Star Edge*, Dec 04 (2020).

McMillan, Sherri. "Focus on the Big Picture for Fitness Business Success." *Club Industry* (2013).

Meyer, Joyce. *Look Great Feel Great: 12 Keys to Enjoying a Healthy Life Now*. New York, New York: Time Warner Book Group, 2006.

Meyer, Vanessa M. 2018. "Sport Psychology for the Soldier Athlete: A Paradigm Shift." *Military Medicine* 183, no. 7-8 (2018): e270-e277.

Michel-Kerjan, Erwann. Effective Risk Response Needs a Prepared Mindset. *Nature (London)*, 517 no. 7535 (2015): 413.

Miller, Andrew. *Mentoring Students and Young People: A Handbook of Effective Practice*. Abingdon, Oxon: Taylor & Francis Group, 2002.

Momon, Kendra. *Being as Leading: Your Roadmap to Shaping Culture Through Life's Disruptions*. Sanford, Florida: AVAIL, 2020.

Montag, Christian, Cornelia Sindermann, David Lester, and Kenneth L. Davis. "Linking Individual Differences in Satisfaction with each of Maslow's Needs to the Big Five

Personality Traits and Panksepp's Primary Emotional Systems." *Heliyon* 6, no. 7 (2020): 1-9.

Moore, Hank. *The Big Picture of Business: Big Ideas and Strategies: 7 Steps Toward Business Success.* (Newburyport: Morgan James Publishing, 2019).

Moore, Kevin. *Wellbeing and Aspirational Culture.* Cham: Springer International Publishing AG, 2019.

Morgan, Gareth. *Images of Organization.* Thousand Oaks, California: Sage Publications, 2006.

Mosca, Joseph B., Alan Fazzari, and John Buzza. "Coaching to Win: A Systematic Approach to Achieving Productivity through Coaching." *Journal of Business & Economics Research* 8, no. 5 (05, 2010): 115-30

Neville, Goddard. *The Power of Imagination.* New York: Tarcher Perigee, 2015.

Northouse. Peter G. *Leadership: Theory and Practice.* Thousand Oaks, California: SAGE Publications, 2016.

Northouse, Peter G. *Leadership: Theory and Practice.* Thousand Oaks, CA: SAGE Publications, 2004, 50-51.

Oster, Gary W. *The Light Prize: Perspectives on Christian Innovation.* Virginia Beach, Virginia: Positive Signs Media, 2011.

Osterwalder, Alexander, and Yves Pigneur. *Business Model Generation: A Handbook for Visionaries, Game Changers, and Challengers.* Hoboken, New Jersey: John Wiley & Sons, Inc., 2010.

Palus, Charles J., and David M. Horth. *The Leader's Edge: Six Creative Compentencies for Navigating Complex Challenges.* San Fancisco, California: John Wiley & Sons, Inc., 2002.

Partnow, Elaine. *The Quotable Woman, Revised Edition: The First 5,000 Years,* Facts on File Library of Language and Literature. New York: Facts on File Inc., 2011.

Peddy, Shirley R. *The Art of Mentoring: Lead, Follow and Get out of the Way* (2nd ed.). Houston, Texas: Bullion Books: 2001.

Percival, Jennifer. "Constructive Feedback." *Nursing Standard* 20 no. 28 (2006): 72.

Peterson, Katie. "Success." *ASAP/Journal* 1, no. 3 (2016): 383.

Pittard, Gary. *Why Winners Win: What it takes to be Successful in Business and Life.* Milton, QLD: John Wiley & Sons, Inc., 2016.

Quote Catalog. 2021. https://quotecatalog.com/quote/peter-tolan-you-know-why-i-8abVdja.

Rapoport, Ron. *See How She Runs: Marion Jones and the Making of a Champion.* Chapel Hill: North Carolina: Algonquin Books, 2000.

Rath, Tom. *Strengths Finder 2.0.* New York, New York: Gallup Press, 2007.

Robson, Sue. *Developing Thinking and Understanding in Young Children: An Introduction for Students.* London: Taylor & Francis, 2006.

Rodgers, Lisa. *Building Positive Momentum for Positive Behavior in Young Children: Strategies for Success in School and Beyond*. London: Jessica Kingsley Publishers, 2018.

Rothwell, William J. *Effective Succession Planning: Ensuring Leadership Continuity and Building Talent from Within*. New York, New York: Amacom, 2016.

Russianoff, Penelope. *When Am I Going to Be Happy: How to Break the Emotional Habits that Make You Miserable*. New York, New York: Bantam Books, 1988.

Sabelskaya. 2022. " Maslow's Pyramid, Hierarchy of Human Needs, Vector Flat Illustration on White Background." Accessed on April 12, 2022. https://www.istockphoto.com/vector/maslows-pyramid-hierarchy-of-human-needs-vector-flat-illustration-on-white-gm1396894083-451501313

Salas-Vallina, Andres and Joaquin Alegre. "Unselfish Leaders? Understanding the Role of Altruistic Leadership and Organizational Learning on Happiness at Work (HAW)." *Leadership & Organization Development Journal* 39, no. 5 (2018): 633-649.

Sanborn, Mark. *The Fred Factor*. New York: Currency, 2004.

Sanders, T. Irene. *Strategic Thinking and the New Science: Planning in the Midst of Chaos, Complexity, and Change*. New York, New York: The Free Press, 1998.

Schultz, Howard, and Dori J. Yang. *Pour Your Heart into it: How Starbucks Built a Company One Cup at a Time*. New York: Hachette Books, 1997.

Sestina, John E. Planning a Successful Future: Managing to Be Wealthy for Individuals and Their Advisors. Hoboken: John Wiley & Sons, Inc., 2016.

Shell, Ellen R. *The Job: Work and its Future in a Time of Radical Change.* New York: Currency, 2018.

Shepherd, Joshua. "Deciding as Intentional Action: Control over Decisions", *Australasian Journal of Philosophy.* 93, no. 2 (2015): 335-351.

Simha, Aditya, and Praveen Parboteeah K. "The Big 5 Personality Traits and Willingness to Justify Unethical Behavior—A Cross-National Examination: JBE." *Journal of Business Ethics*: 1-21 (2019): 1-21.

Stein, Steven J. *The EQ Leader: Instilling Passion, Creating Shared Goals, and Building Meaningful Organizations through Emotional Intelligence.* New York: Wiley, 2017.

Stevenson, Robert L. AZ Quotes. https://www.azquotes.com/quotes/topics/maps.html, n.d.

Stuz, Phil, and Barry Michels. *The Tools: 5 Tools to Help You Find Courage, Creativity, and Willpower-and Inspire You to Live in Forward Motion.* New York: Spriegel & Grau Trade Paperbacks, 2012.

"Success Done Right; Chick-fil-A is one of the Country's Most Successful Quick-service

Chains, and it Still Focuses on Quality Food and Community Service", 2008, *US business review,* [Online], 9, no. 9 (2008): 172-174.

Seuss, Dr. *Oh the Places You'll Go!* New York: Random House, 1990.

Tansey, Stephen D. *Business, Information Technology and Society.* New York, New York: Routledge, 2003.

Tracy, Brian. *No Excuses! The Power of Self-discipline.* New York: MJF Books, 2010.

Trowbridge, Terry. "The Blind Locksmith." *The Mathematical Intelligencer* 41, no. 4 (2019):16.

Van Den Born, Arjan, and Arjen Van Witteloostuijn. "Drivers of Freelance Career Success." *Journal of Organizational Behavior* 34, no. 1 (2013): 24-46.

Veith Jr., Gene E. *God at Work: Your Christian Vocation in All of Life.* Wheaton, Illinois: Crossway, 2002.

Vickmanis, Laura, & Amy Sohn. *It's Not about the Pom-Poms: How a 40-year-old Mom Became the NFL's Oldest Cheerleader.* New York: Random House, 2012.

Walton, David. *Emotional Intelligence: A Practical Guide.* New York, New York: MJF Books, 2012.

Warren, Rick. *The Purpose Driven Life: What on Earth am I Here For?* Grand Rapids, MI: Zondervan, 2002.

Weber, Eric T. "Self-Respect and a Sense of Positive Power: On Protection, Self-Affirmation, and Harm in the Charge of "Acting White"." *The Journal of Speculative Philosophy* 30, no. 1 (2016): 45-63.

Woolfe, Lorin. *Leadership Secrets from The Bible: From Moses to Matthew: Management Lessons for Contemporary*

Leaders. New York: MJF Books Fine Communications, 2002.

Younger, Mike, and Molly Warrington. "Mentoring and Target-Setting in a Secondary School in England: An Evaluation of Aims and Benefits." *Oxford Review of Education* 35, no. 2 (2009): 177.

Yuill, Nicola, and Sarah Little. "Thinking or Feeling? an Exploratory Study of Maternal Scaffolding, Child Mental State Talk, and Emotion Understanding in Language-impaired and Typically Developing School-aged Children." *British Journal of Educational Psychology* 88, no. 2 (2018): 261-283.

INDEX

A

accomplishment 35

   and achievement (success) 34-35, 59-60, 132-133

   and choices 33

achieve (*success*). *See* success achievers

affirmations 3, 54-56, 119, 153

   in research 113-114

B

BHAGS (big, hairy, audacious, goals) 26

bragging. *See* Bragging Factor

Bragging Factor 20-21, 57, 120

benchmark(s) 49, 63, 96

   in research 105, 109, 112,

C

coach (coaching) 9, 93-94, 135, 139, 144-146, 149, 155

   in research 108

   versus mentorship 147-149

correction 89, 95. *Also see* self-correction

cultural

and behavior 27, 43
and success 94
influences 14, 21, 43
   in research 100, 112, 115, 119-120
norms, 14-15

D

decision (decisions)
   and behavior 32
   and leader development 122
   and Master Key 40, 55. *Also see* Master Key
   and success 9, 40-43, 46, 138-139
drivers
   internal 7, 27-28
   success 16, 33-34
   and humanistic needs 67

E

environmental
   factors 13
      and limitations 41-42, 49, 96-97
      and mentors 140-141, 155
      and positive influences 50-55, 62, 72, 96-97, 112, 119, 122, 131
      and success 13-15, 17, 24, 35 58, 60-62, 93-94, 122
      and skill development 84-85, 94
      in research 99-102, 112, 115, 117
ethics
   and performance 141-142

LeaderMind Model 62-63, 115

logotherapy 18-19

M

Maslow's Hierarchy of Needs, 16-17, 70

Master Key

  and decisions 39-40, 49, 55

  and goal setting 135

  and imposter syndrome 56-57

  and visualization 138

  applied (exercise) 42, 56, 156

Master Key Thinking

  theory 7

  defined 39-40

mental

  capacity 3, 114

  focus 4, 6, 8, 20, 26-28

    and behavior 64-66

    in action 87

  fortitude (stamina) 26, 64-66, 74, 88, 99, 120, 122-123, 125, 156

    and habits 153. *Also see* habit (mental fortitude)

    in research 112, 114

  growth 7, 66

Mental Mogul Mindset. *See* mindset *(mental mogul)*

Mental Moments *(exercises)* 26-28, 42-43, 57-58, 74-75, 88, 98, 123, 138, 149-150

mentor (mentors, mentoring, mentorship) 9, 20, 64, 100, 135, 140-144, 155

  and *LeaderMind* pillars 64, 122

R

S

Self
  self-actualization 16, 24-25, 70
  self-care 8, 80, 89-92
  self-confidence 20-23, 141
  self-control 31-32, 49
  self-correction 8
    and mistakes 97
  self-discipline 23, 34
  self-discovery 18-19. *Also see* logotherapy
  self-image 7, 27
  self-intrusive 17. *Also see* hedonistic
  self-worth 50, 57, 71
skill-building 83-85, 89, 93, 154
social contexts 14
success achievers
  achieving success 25-26, 34-35
  and change 27, 33, 72, 128
  and giving 18, 22, 71-72
  and fear 22
  and progress 24-25
Success Behaviors Research 101-123

T

toolkit(s) 8, 77-98, 156
training 79, 123, 154
  and culture 73
  and coaching 148
  and *LeaderMind* 63-64, 101

www.ingramcontent.com/pod-product-compliance
Lightning Source LLC
Chambersburg PA
CBHW051150120626
46547CB00012B/1030